Stories Untold Productions presents

ODE TO JOY

(How Gordon got to go to the nasty pig party)

by James Ley

First preview at Platform, Glasgow on 21 July 2022

First performance at Summerhall for the Edinburgh
Festival Fringe on 3 August 2022

Company List

Cast
Gordon	Brian Evans
Cumpig/ Marcus	Sean Connor
Manpussy/ Tom	Marc Mackinnon

Creative Team
Writer / Director	James Ley
Dramaturg	Rosie Kellagher
Assistant Director	Matt McBrier
DJ	Simon 'Simonotron' Eilbeck
Movement Director	Craig Manson
Sound Designer	Susan Bear
Lighting Designer	Emma Jones
Costume Designer	Cleo Rose McCabe
Wardrobe Assistant	Hana Eggleston

Production Team
Production Manager	Simon Gane
Stage Manager	Jordan Alsoudani
Show Technician	Chris Gorman

Produced by Stories Untold Productions Ltd
Producer	Robyn Jancovich-Brown
Assistant Producer	Kirsten McPake

Created with support from Creative Scotland and Platform, Glasgow. Written on attachment to National Theatre of Scotland. Part of the 2022 Made in Scotland Showcase at Edinburgh Festival Fringe.

Company Biographies

Brian Evans – Gordon

Brian Evans trained in Drama and Performance at Queen Margaret University in Edinburgh and graduated in 2021. With a passion for queer theatre, Brian is proud to be making his professional Fringe debut as Gordon in *Ode to Joy (How Gordon got to go to the nasty pig party)*. Brian's recent stage credits include: *The Gathering* (Beacon Arts Centre), *Widows*, *Blue Stockings* (West College Scotland), *Animal Farm* (City of Glasgow College).

Sean Connor – Cumpig/Marcus

Sean Connor is an actor based in Glasgow, Scotland. He graduated from New College Lanarkshire with a Bachelor of Arts (Hons) in Acting in 2017, and has since appeared in numerous film and television projects, including *Schemers* (Black Factory Films, 2020), *Still Game* (BBC1, 2019), *Anna and the Apocalypse* (Vertigo Films, 2017). He also played series regular Dylan Christie in the hit BBC Scotland show *River City*, and most recently made his debut theatre performance playing the role of Paul in the critically acclaimed *Moorcroft* at the Tron Theatre.

Marc Mackinnon – Manpussy/Tom

Marc is a Scottish actor based in London and Edinburgh. He completed his undergraduate at University of Glasgow before training at Mountview, graduating in 2017. Recent credits include: *Four Play* (Above The Stag); *Peter Gynt* (National Theatre); *Blithe Spirit*, *Measure For Measure* (Changeling Theatre Company); *Metropolis* (Old Rose & Crown Theatre); *Daisy, Like the Flower* (Theatre N16).

James Ley – Writer/Director

James is a playwright living in Glasgow. *Ode to Joy (How Gordon got to go to the nasty pig party)* is his directorial debut. As a writer, his plays include *Wilf* (Traverse Theatre), *Love Song to Lavender Menace* (Royal Lyceum Theatre Edinburgh, Summerhall, SoHo Playhouse/New York), *Emma and Gill* (Catherine Wheels, Lung Ha), *I Heart Maths* (A Play, a Pie and a Pint) and *Spain* (Glasgay!, Citizens Theatre). James was Writer on Attachment to National Theatre of Scotland in 2022 and he was selected for the 2019 Edinburgh International Film Festival Talent Lab and the 2019 Stowe Story Labs in Vermont, USA. His feature adaptation of *Love Song to Lavender Menace* is in development, produced by John McKay/Compact Pictures, funded by the Scottish Film Talent Network.

Rosie Kellagher – Dramaturg

Rosie Kellagher is Dramaturg at National Theatre of Scotland and has previously worked as Literary Associate at the Traverse, Liverpool Everyman and Playhouse and Live Theatre in Newcastle. As a freelance dramaturg and award-winning director she has made work for both theatre and radio with companies across the UK and beyond including Traverse Theatre, Soho Theatre, BBC, Vanishing Point, The Arches, Dance City, Live Theatre, Arcola Theatre and Riksteatern, Sweden.

Matt McBrier – Assistant Director

Matt McBrier is an Edinburgh-based queer, working-class Scottish theatre artist. He holds a BA (Hons) Performance from Mountview, and a Masters of Fine Arts in Directing from Edinburgh Napier University, tutored under former artistic director of The Lyceum, Mark Thomson. Matt is interested in socially motivated projects, new writing, facilitating performance education and participation. Projects Matt has directed include *Crossing Care* by Kirin Saeed and Sara Garcia Pereda, a Creative Scotland-funded production for World Vision Day 2020, and performance art piece Anuna by Elise Steenackers at the Talbot Rice Gallery.

Simon 'Simonotron' Eilbeck – DJ

Simon has been a radio and nightclub DJ for 26 years. In 2010, he started Hot Mess, the longest-running queer dance party in Scotland, which takes place every month at Sneaky Pete's in Edinburgh and the Poetry Club in Glasgow. His monthly Hot Mess radio show can be heard on Clyde Built Radio. Acting credits include Alasdair Gray's *McGrotty and Ludmilla* (HATS), *The Idiot at the Wall* (Stoirm Òg) and *Blackadder Goes Forth* (Edinburgh People's Theatre). In 2019, Simon's essay 'Let's Go Swimming: One Man's Reflections on Being Gay and Bisexual' was published in Monstrous Regiment's *The Bi-ble: New Testimonials*.

Craig Manson - Movement Director

Craig Manson is a performance artist and performer whose work spans theatre, live art, dance, film, cabaret and club performance. His work uses humour and movement to explore contemporary queer themes, often working in collaboration with other LGBTQIA+ artists to create exhilarating experiences for an audience. In 2022 he was selected to be part of the Made in Scotland showcase for his show *GAYBOYS* at Summerhall from 16–28 August. Previous work has been presented in association with Tramway, Southbank Centre, CCA, Buzzcut, The Yard, Camden People's Theatre and Scottee.

Susan Bear – Sound Designer

Susan Bear (she/her) is a multi-instrumentalist, sound designer, composer and artist working across the mediums of music, theatre, games and advertising. Bear has a proven track record of excellence and versatility in composition, production, mixing and musical arrangement through a variety of projects for both commercial and grassroots organisations.

Recent composition and sound design projects include *Wilf* (Traverse Theatre), the Scotgov NHS 'Roll Up Your Sleeves' advertising campaign, composition and sound design for mobile game *Journey to the End of the Jelly World*, composition and musical arrangement for Civic Digit's *Big Data Show*, as well as audio for the accompanying mobile app; sound design and composition for *Hope & Joy* (Stellar Quines); sound design for National Theatre of Scotland's *Dear Europe*, as well as various other compositional work for other Scottish theatre companies.

Bear has toured internationally with bands such as Tuff Love, The Pastels, Malcolm Middleton, Pictish Trail, Tracyanne & Danny, as well as performing in and touring the Fringe First-winning production of *What Girls Are Made Of* (Cora Bissett/Orla O'Loughlin) as an actor and musician. Her second solo album, *Alter*, entirely written, played, produced, recorded and mixed by Susan was released June 10th 2022 on Lost Map Records.

Over the last year Susan has been songwriting and producing music with Scottish all-female & non-binary collective Hen Hoose. She has previously been involved in organising, teaching and mentoring at Girls Rock Glasgow, a DIY rock camp for young girls teaching confidence, music-making and creativity.

Simon Gane – Production Manager

Simon is a freelance Designer and Production Manager based in the beautiful North East of Scotland. He trained in his hometown at the Bristol Old Vic as a Technician a few more years ago than he now cares to remember. He worked as a venue-based Technical Manager for many years, notably at TIC TOC in Coventry and The Lemon Tree in Aberdeen, where he was also resident Lighting Designer. He then toured with a number of bands as Sound Engineer. Since leaving the world of a secure salary to forge a more creative path, Simon has been realising productions nationally and internationally; inside, outside, and site-specific; and running shows at the Fringe alongside the full Dance Base program at Scotland's National Centre for Dance. He has built four Fringe venues and was once Technical Manager for a 32-shows day: all good prep for helping James and *Ode to Joy* achieve the potential out of the kit, time and experience for this run at Summerhall.

Emma Jones – Lighting Designer
Emma is a Lighting Designer based in Scotland, working across the UK and abroad. Emma has lit shows for numerous companies including Dundee Rep Theatre, Perth Theatre, Derby Theatre, Scottish Dance Theatre, Stellar Quines, The National Theatre of Scotland, The Royal Lyceum Edinburgh, Catherine Wheels Theatre Company and The Citizens Theatre Glasgow. Recently Emma has started collaborating with music artist SHHE. Emma has designed the lighting for over 16 newly commissioned works for Scottish Dance Theatre, working with both established and emerging choreographers including Damien Jalet, Anton Lachky, Botis Seva and Henri Oguike. In 2020 Emma became an associate artist with Shotput Theatre Company. 2022 shows so far include: *LENA – The Lena Zavaroni Story* for Feather Productions, *Lightning Ridge* for Catherine Wheels Theatre Company, *Ray* for Scottish Dance Theatre and *The Emperor's New Clothes*, a co-production between Derby Theatre, Hiccup Theatre and Polka Theatre. Other shows at this year's Fringe include *Antigone, Interrupted* for Scottish Dance Theatre, *And* by Charlotte McLean and *DYRA* by SHHE.

Cleo Rose McCabe – Costume Designer
Cleo is an Edinburgh-based professional costume designer and maker. She has more than ten years' experience, specialising in dance, circus, masks, drag, cabaret and animal costumes.

Hana Eggleston – Wardrobe Assistant
Hana Eggleston is an aspiring costume maker and designer, halfway through an HND in Costume for Stage and Screen at Edinburgh College. So far she has made stagewear for drag queens, assisted on an international Whitney Houston tribute tour, and made a whole heap of period garments and fancy dress.

Stories

Stories Untold Productions Ltd

Founded in 2021, Stories Untold Productions is a new Scotland-based production company focusing on work which promotes equality, inclusion and well-being in society.

Stories Untold Productions seeks to speak about the unspoken and highlight stories and voices which are not heard in mainstream spaces. They are creative producers who work collaboratively with artists to research, create, stage and tour work which challenges the systemic under-representation of particular artists and topics on local, national and international stages.

James Ley

Ode to Joy

(How Gordon got to go to the nasty pig party)

Salamander Street

PLAYS

Published in 2022 by Salamander Street Ltd,
272 Bath Street, Glasgow, G2 4JR (info@salamanderstreet.com).

Ode to Joy (How Gordon got to go to the nasty pig party) © James Ley 2022.
All rights reserved.

PB ISBN: 9781914228681

10 9 8 7 6 5 4 3 2 1

Further copies of this publication can be purchased from
www.salamanderstreet.com

For Wayne Shelby

Characters

MANPUSSY

CUMPIG

GORDON

… means they don't finish what they're saying

/ means they get cut off by a line or an action

An intense techno set is playing in the turbine hall of Berghain nightclub – a mess of bodies, sex and sportswear.

In the midst of it all is **CUMPIG** *– joyously dancing and coming up on something. At the edge of the party is* **GORDON** *– nervous, sweating and dressed in office wear.*

As the music becomes super-chaotic, **MANPUSSY** *rushes in, wearing a riot of things he's bought at the airport and Irish jig shoes. He's holding a butt plug. He speaks to us:*

MANPUSSY: Ok…

                  So…

                  Fuck…

                  Ok…

                  So…

MANPUSSY *puts the butt plug up to his lips and speaks into it. The butt plug successfully amplifies* **MANPUSSY** *but makes him German:*

MANPUSSY: So!

                  [So!]

                  Es war einmal!

                  [Once upon a time!]

                  Es war einmal!

He stops using the butt plug and shouts.

MANPUSSY: Once upon a time!

                  There was a beautiful narrator!

                  Called Manpussy!

                  Manpussy didn't get into Berghain tonight!

                  Oh fuck!

The music gets louder.

MANPUSSY:	Manpussy didn't get into Berghain tonight because he wasn't wearing sportswear, so he came in as the narrator!
	And look, it worked!
	Ta da!
	(Into the butt plug.)
	Hier bin ich!
	[Here I am!]
	Hier bin ich!

MANPUSSY *drops the butt plug and stretches out his arms.*

MANPUSSY:	Here I am!
CUMPIG:	Manpussy!
MANPUSSY:	Cumpig!
CUMPIG:	What the fuck is going on?
MANPUSSY:	I didn't get in.
CUMPIG:	Well you're here now, that's the main thing.
MANPUSSY:	I'm not here now.
	I didn't get in.
	I've had to come in as the narrator.
	(Beat.)
	How am I doing?
CUMPIG:	You're fucking nailing it.
MANPUSSY:	Yeah?
CUMPIG:	Yeah, you're my favourite narrator.
MANPUSSY:	And you're my favourite person.
CUMPIG:	Come on!

Let's go and get fucked by strangers!

MANPUSSY: Wait!

Where's Gordon?

CUMPIG: I don't know.

He's… somewhere.

(Beat.)

Let's check out the 16-man piss pool.

CUMPIG *rushes towards the sex action area.*

MANPUSSY: Cumpig, no, I can't.

I'm the narrator.

I have to… tell the story.

CUMPIG: What story?

MANPUSSY: This story!

(To us.) Once upon a time a few days ago,

My husband and I are at a sex party in a hotel room in Malmaison.

CUMPIG: Are we?

MANPUSSY: Yes!

We've been here for days.

CUMPIG: We've been here for 22 hours max.

MANPUSSY: Who's Max?

'Me' says a voice in the corner.

Oh look, it's Max from Morningside getting fucked by everyone at the sex party.

Hiya Max!

CUMPIG: You go gurl!

MANPUSSY:	I'm lying on the floor with a tube of Pringles in my ass.
	Sour cream and chive.
CUMPIG:	Why?
MANPUSSY:	Because Gonz is putting a golf ball into it from the bed.
	Gonz is standing on the bed, lining up a golf ball with his putter.
	Gonz was here on business from Spain and was playing golf with clients.
	Doggybagz, Federico and Hamish have taken a break from nipple torture to watch.
	Cumpig was on his phone, or he would have filmed it.
	Gonz putts the ball across the bed.
	The golf ball lands on the coffee table,
	And rolls along the spine of Gonz's copy of *Troubled Blood* by Robert Galbraith.
CUMPIG:	What's with all the details?
MANPUSSY:	Just kind of makes it more believable.
	The ball spins off the edge of the table,
	Passes the lip of the Pringles tube and drops inside me.
	I'm a hole in one.
CUMPIG:	Fuck yeah!

CUMPIG *snorts something off his finger and offers some to* **MANPUSSY**.

MANPUSSY:	Where did you get that?

CUMPIG *shrugs and hands* **MANPUSSY** *a baggy. It's empty.*

MANPUSSY:	Where's Gordon?

GORDON *turns. He's cunted and gurning.*

GORDON: I am so sorry.

MANPUSSY: Jesus, Gordon.

GORDON: I'm sorry.

MANPUSSY: Save it.

Listen, Gordon, I didn't get in.

GORDON: Well you're here now, and that's the main thing.

MANPUSSY: I'm not here, I've had to come in as the narrator.

GORDON: Listen, I might go home.

MANPUSSY: You can't.

GORDON: I can, I'm scared.

MANPUSSY: No, you're excited.

You're walking along the corridor of the Malmaison.

It's a week ago.

You straighten your tie.

GORDON: I don't wear a tie.

MANPUSSY: Gordon!

GORDON: Oh, this tie!

GORDON *mimes straightening his tie.*

MANPUSSY: And action!

There's a knock at the door.

GORDON *knocks on an imaginary door.*

MANPUSSY: Cumpig goes to answer it.

CUMPIG *goes to answer it.*

MANPUSSY: Don't answer it!

CUMPIG: You just told me to answer it.

MANPUSSY: I was narrating and then I jumped back to now.

And now I need to give Gordon's backstory.

(To us.) Cumpig had found Gordon on an app.

CUMPIG: Show me your hole.

GORDON: My bum hole?

CUMPIG: Aye.

MANPUSSY: Their chat was quite basic.

It was 7pm but Gordon was still at work.

He'd never been invited to a chem sex party before.

GORDON: Wait, am I being invited to a chem sex party?

CUMPIG: Yes, show me your hole.

GORDON: I'm not going to show someone my hole, that's disgusting.

MANPUSSY: Then someone Gordon had spooned with two weeks ago walked past his desk.

The big spoon.

GORDON: All I ever do is spooning, with guys with Prince Charming energy.

MANPUSSY: Thought Gordon.

Then suddenly he stood up from his desk and shouted:

GORDON: I don't want to meet Prince Charming and I'm not a fucking kitchen utensil!

MANPUSSY: Gordon had a semi which he covered with…

GORDON *produces a sweaty document from his shorts.*

GORDON: My copy of the 'Brexit impact study draft seven with Brenda's amends.'

MANPUSSY:	Gordon went to the accessible toilet, pulled down his pants and/
GORDON:	Really bad pants, sorry.
MANPUSSY:	He pulled down his really bad pants and/
GORDON:	I can't do this.
	I'm Gordon.

GORDON *retreats back into the nightclub.*

MANPUSSY:	Gordon, you can.
	You have to.
GORDON:	I'm gonna go outside for a bit.
MANPUSSY:	No!
GORDON:	You can't tell me what to do.
MANPUSSY:	I can, I'm…

MANPUSSY *flies up to the ceiling, floating in the air and producing a divine shaft of light.* **GORDON** *turns. He and* **CUMPIG** *are both blinded by the light.*

MANPUSSY:	I'm God.
GORDON:	How did you do that?
MANPUSSY:	I don't know.
CUMPIG:	When did you get so high?
MANPUSSY:	When I became God.
GORDON:	I don't believe in God.
MANPUSSY:	Now you do, Bitch, says God,
	You could be having so much fun, like the others.
GORDON:	What others?
MANPUSSY:	All the other gays.
GORDON:	I'm not like all the other gays, I'm Gordon!

MANPUSSY:	Oh come on, all the gays are the same.
	You could have a hospital mask attached to a bottle of poppers on your bedside table.
	You could have a cabinet in your room filled with big latex dicks.
GORDON:	How do you know I don't?
MANPUSSY:	Because I know everything.
	You don't even own a butt plug, do you?
GORDON:	Yes.
	No.
	I don't know.
	Maybe I... fist myself?
MANPUSSY:	Do you?
GORDON:	No.
MANPUSSY:	Why not?
	Two fingers good, four fingers bad?
GORDON:	I'd never thought of it like that.
MANPUSSY:	Well that's the point of a divine intervention, to change what you think.
	Now come to Malmaison and get your hoop in the air.
GORDON:	I can't, I'm Gordon.
MANPUSSY:	Then stop being Gordon.
	You can be whoever you want to be.
GORDON:	That's not true!
MANPUSSY:	Calm down.
GORDON:	It's not true.

(To us.)

When I was writing my part of the Brexit impact study I came across the philosopher David Hume.

MANPUSSY: You don't have this kind of relationship with the audience.

GORDON: *(Ignoring **MANPUSSY**.)* Hume said that the self is a fiction.

The whole notion of personal and national boundaries are fictitious.

Individualism is/

MANPUSSY: Oh shut up and take a photo of your bum hole.

GORDON: No.

MANPUSSY: Gordon bent over in the Scottish Government toilets and took tons of pictures of his nasty hole.

He sent the best one to Cumpig.

Cumpig loves bum holes.

CUMPIG: Loves!

MANPUSSY: And that's how Cumpig and Gordon met.

GORDON: And I'm really sorry guys, but this is how Gordon and Cumpig part.

CUMPIG: I don't think so.

GORDON: I'm sorry.

GORDON *starts to retreat into the club.*

CUMPIG: Bring that furry bum hole to Malmaison!

GORDON: Ok.

GORDON *rushes back on.*

CUMPIG: Great, where are you?

GORDON:	I'm at the office.
CUMPIG:	Nice, are you wearing a suit?
GORDON:	Yes, kind of, well smart casual, it's/
CUMPIG:	Nice, do roleplay.
GORDON:	Sure.
CUMPIG:	Can I load you?
GORDON:	Yeah.
CUMPIG:	I'm undetectable, is that ok?
GORDON:	Fine.
MANPUSSY:	Gordon had never done roleplay before or been loaded but he was on prep.
	He'd lied to get it.
	He told the nurse at the gum clinic/
GORDON:	I like to lie on the kitchen table, blindfolded, with the door on the snib taking loads for days.
	Days and days.
	(Aside.) Completely made up.
MANPUSSY:	Suddenly Gordon is in the Malmaison lobby, clutching the 'Brexit impact study' with no idea what to do for role play.
	But then he sees…
GORDON:	A waiter coming from the brasserie and I think of something that will be absolutely tits funny dot org!
MANPUSSY:	There's a knock at the door.

GORDON *goes back to his position knocking on the door.*

CUMPIG:	Now?
MANPUSSY:	Yes!

CUMPIG *mimes opening the door.*

GORDON: Burger!

I mean room service!

I mean – hi!

I mean shoot me!

I mean – bye!

MANPUSSY: What were you thinking?

GORDON: I was being room service.

MANPUSSY: You have an actual burger.

GORDON: Oh my god, I have an actual burger.

Who the fuck am I?

MANPUSSY: Mortified, Gordon turns to leave.

CUMPIG: That arse!

MANPUSSY: Thinks Cumpig.

CUMPIG: Gordon, wait!

MANPUSSY: Gordon turns his arse and face to Cumpig.

GORDON *tries to do this.*

MANPUSSY: Cumpig loves a posh boy gone pig more than anything.

GORDON: I'm not posh, I'm worthless.

CUMPIG: Oh, who cares if you're posh or not, get naked.

MANPUSSY: Gordon strips and makes really shit conversation.

GORDON *is about to strip but stops himself and mimes stripping instead.*

GORDON: I do, I have verbal diarrhoea.

But that's the only diarrhoea I have, I can assure you.

	Did I say that out loud, Cumpig?
CUMPIG:	Yes.
GORDON:	Cumpig's a great name.
CUMPIG:	Manpussy gave me that name.
	Because I'm a cum junkie.
MANPUSSY:	He's a junkie junkie.
	Same with everything.
	Skittles.
CUMPIG:	CrossFit.
MANPUSSY:	Meth.
CUMPIG:	Cum.
MANPUSSY:	Red Wine.
CUMPIG:	The Sopranos.
GORDON:	Maybe I should have a sex name.
MANPUSSY:	Maybe it's not all about you.
GORDON:	It feels like it is.
	This feels like my story.
MANPUSSY:	I've just had to make it about you to get us out of this mess.
GORDON:	I'm so sorry guys.
MANPUSSY:	Doesn't matter, keep it going.
GORDON:	The Malmaison hotel room blows my mind.
	It reeks of sex.
	There must be twenty-five guys here.
MANPUSSY:	There's eight.

GORDON:	It's dark and seedy and I want to be part of it.
MANPUSSY:	Give Cumpig more of that bad chat and get involved.
GORDON:	Gordon doesn't really mean anything, Cumpig.
	Well it does.
	It means spacious fort.
	But I mean… what does that mean?
	(Beat.)
	I know, I wouldn't have anything to say to that either.
MANPUSSY:	Says Gordon, as he climbs on the bed,
	Spreading his cheeks in a clinical way.
	Oh wow!
	Gordon really does have a lovely hole.
CUMPIG:	Told you.
MANPUSSY:	Yes, but his chat, my fucking god.
GORDON:	Breach my boundaries!
	Redefine the male body politic!
	Make my leak!
	Cum inside my hostile environment!
MANPUSSY:	Jesus Christ.
GORDON:	When you imagine yourself at a sex party,
	you're really imaging someone else at sex party…
	But this is me at a sex party, isn't it?
CUMPIG:	Yes, just super posh.
GORDON:	I'm not posh, I just come across that way.
	I'm like Ferrero Rocher.

	Did I say that out loud?
MANPUSSY:	Yes, you did.
	It's hilarious.
GORDON:	Oh my word, I'm just me at a sexy party.
	And it doesn't work, does it?
MANPUSSY:	I love it.
	It's the funniest thing I've ever seen.
CUMPIG:	Where's ma baggie?
GORDON:	What?
CUMPIG:	I'm looking for my wee bag of Tina!
	Where is it?
GORDON:	I don't have it.
	I don't need drugs to have a good time.
	Did I say that out loud?
MANPUSSY:	Yes, you say it kind of seductively to Big Stevie.
	That's when Gonz tells you it's time to leave.
GORDON:	What?
	I didn't even mean that.
	I'm chem friendly – hi!
	I've done a lot of poppers...
	And I mean a lot...
	I was fucked up on that shit!
MANPUSSY:	Gordon gets off the bed, standing on Gonz's foot again.
GORDON:	I am soooo sorry.

MANPUSSY:	He puts his pants on, falling over like a slapstick… person.
GORDON:	I can't find my socks.
MANPUSSY:	Forget your socks.
GORDON:	I've done a lot of gross things this afternoon but I'm not about to wear shoes without socks.
MANPUSSY:	Gordon grabs Cumpig's red football socks I gifted him at Leeds Pig Weekend.
GORDON:	Do they have a pig weekend in Leeds?
CUMPIG:	Yeah, it's just in people's hooses but it's nasty.
MANPUSSY:	Gordon flees.
	And then as he waited for the lift it hit him.
CUMPIG:	The lift?
MANPUSSY:	No.
GORDON:	Oh my fucking God, Cumpig wanted me and I fucked it up.
MANPUSSY:	The lift wasn't coming so he took the stairs.
GORDON:	I'm an arsehole.
MANPUSSY:	A very long spiral staircase.
GORDON:	A total cunt.
MANPUSSY:	He's like a Disney princess.
GORDON:	I hate my life.

CUMPIG *picks up* **GORDON**'s *report.*

CUMPIG:	Oh fuck he's left his…
	(Reads.) Brexit impact study report draft 7 with Brenda's amends.

MANPUSSY:	Cumpig throws his clothes on and chases after Gordon,
	Taking the stairs in fours and fives.
	On the steps of Malmaison,
	Just as the sunset was turning the undersides of the clouds electric magenta,
	Gordon disappeared over the old railway bridge.
CUMPIG:	He's gone.
MANPUSSY:	Then I emerge from Malmaison, like a glistening cum goddess.
CUMPIG:	Manpussy, he's deleted his Grindr.
	I have no way to contact him.
MANPUSSY:	Good, get in the Uber.

CUMPIG *mimes getting in the Uber.* **MANPUSSY** *grabs the report off* **CUMPIG** *and reads it:*

MANPUSSY:	Gordon has been part of a project looking at the devastating impact of Brexit.
GORDON:	They put me in a focus group at work a few weeks ago.
	The focus was: the fallout of Brexit and its impact on art and culture.
	I got put in an LGBTQ working group.
	I took: what are LGBTQ night clubs and parties, niche and fetish?
	I mean I have been to night clubs and parties before
	But I'm not like Frank from Fiscal Sustainability.
	Frank never works on Mondays.
	And you don't get two words out of him on Tuesdays.
	The research blew my mind.

I discovered a whole world I knew nothing about.

And that there is almost no limit to what you can put in your arsehole.

My research led me to SNAX.

MANPUSSY: *(To us.)* My favourite sleazy pig party.

GORDON: SNAX started in the late 90s.

CUMPIG: I fucking love SNAX.

GORDON: It quickly became a favourite in Berlin, for its hardcore techno parties, where club-goers were free to act on their desires in a private space.

They could be themselves, without fear of judgement.

Then in 1998 the SNAX founders found a home for it in an old train repairs factory on the banks of the Spree.

In their new home the SNAX parties gave birth to the legendary underground club Ostgut.

Ostgut welcomed gay men and club kids to dance to the latest techno.

MANPUSSY: Some nights at Ostgut entire rooms would be filled with mud.

GORDON: Naked guys danced around, having sex with each other and acting like pigs.

In 2003 Ostgut vanished when the site was cleared by the government to make way for a sports stadium.

MANPUSSY: SNAX and Ostgut were sent into space, orbiting East Berlin, looking for somewhere to manifest.

Then on the 15th of October 2004, the ball of light and darkness and energy saw exactly what it was looking for.

GORDON: A huge disused power station!

MANPUSSY:	The ball of energy came crashing to earth, smashing through the 20-metre ceilings of the power station/
	Steel and concrete was ripped apart to make way for...
	A Funktion-One sound system.
	Berghain was born.

GORDON *dances in his bedroom.*

MANPUSSY:	People came to Berghain from all over the world.
	Drawn in by the deep, dark base tones that seep through the thick walls of the old East German power plant,
	Like the aroma escaping from a chocolate factory.
GORDON:	Once a year, at the Easter weekend, the SNAX club returns to Berghain,
	Bringing with it a no-holds barred gay sex party to nearly die for.

GORDON *is excited now and he's really frenetically dancing.*

GORDON:	Reading about SNAX threw me into turmoil.
	Sex has never been a big part of me.
	But I'm only twenty-seven.
	Am I judging myself?
	Is spooning my sentence?
	Netflix and kill me now?
	I don't like who I am!
	(Beat.)
	So I created PG.
	Pig Gordon; my alter ego.

PG likes to have dicks slapping off of his face and takes anonymous loads from strangers…

Off his tits on…

I researched it:

Crystal meth which makes you really horny for hours, days, weeks.

G, which is more of a subtle high but lethal if you go slightly over the required dose.

Ketamine, which makes the other drugs last longer,

Speed,

Coke,

E,

Mandy.

For weeks PG was trapped in my head.

And I don't know how to get him to come out.

But then I discovered Techno Bunker.

The music gets really sleazy and exciting. **GORDON** *feels it and dances to it.*

GORDON: Techno Bunker is a Spotify playlist.

Constantly updated, it plays dark, sick, sleazy tunes.

And it turns out… I love it.

And it gives me a connection to sex.

Real sex.

Because at any moment chem sex parties across the world are tuning in.

(Beat.)

At home I can't sleep/

So I go to the kitchen to make a herbal tea,

And stuck to my fridge is my ticket for SNAX 2022.

I hold it to my face, sniff it, and imagine the smell of…
body fluids.

Then I hold the top edge of the paper, between my
fingers and/

MANPUSSY: Across the universe in another part of Leith,

Cumpig had just found Gordon's email address.

CUMPIG: Oh look – it's on the front of his report.

MANPUSSY: Cumpig got his phone out and composed a missive of
Shakespearean brilliance:

CUMPIG: Hi Gordon,

You've got a really nice furry bum hole man.

Peach.

Chocolate donut.

I wanted to load it.

Dribble face.

Squirt.

Peach.

I'm gutted you went.

I would have ate it.

Tongue.

Squirt.

Yum.

I've lost my chems.

Pill, Syringe, cry face.

Did you go off with my socks?

Socks.

You sniffing them now and fingering yourself?

Point right.

Chocolate donut.

Nose.

Dribble face.

You nasty boy.

I've got your Brexit impact study draft 7 with Brenda's amends.

I think she's missing the point to be honest.

She's focusing too much on fiscal policy.

And you're right, the cultural impact goes deeper than economics.

Tragedy face comedy face money bag.

Anyway, you dropped it on the floor when you offered your chocolate donut to all the:

Pig face.

Pig face.

Pig face.

Come to my gym tomorrow and I'll give it to you.

The report that is.

Pig face.

Squat.

Running.

Bring ma socks.

If you find my Tina, bring that too.

Diamond.

Maybe I'll squirt in your chocolate donut tongue devil peach squirt pill syringe heart.

Cumpig/Marcus.

Squirt.

Pig nose.

Crazy face.

Kiss heart kiss heart crazy face pig nose.

MANPUSSY: Cumpig sent the email to legal at scot dot gov.

CUMPIG: Gordon's like the lawyer for the whole of the Scottish Government.

He's a clever cunt.

MANPUSSY: Actually he wasn't the lawyer for Scottish Government,

He was one of 250 lawyers for the Scottish Government who all had access to the group mailbox.

Back at Gordon's, he'd calmed down.

He kissed the ticket, stuck it back on the fringe and sighed.

SNAX was tomorrow but he wouldn't be there.

Gordon walked back to his bedroom,

Clutching a mug of tea that said 'SUGAR TITS'.

Then as he entered the room a perverted track from Boris, his favourite Berghain DJ came on Techno Bunker.

"Alexa!" said Gordon.

He was about to say 'stop', but he stopped himself and:

GORDON: Alexa, turn it up.

MANPUSSY: Gordon danced.

GORDON *dances.*

MANPUSSY: Gordon danced.

GORDON *dances.*

MANPUSSY: As Gordon danced,

250 lawyers read Cumpig's email.

As Gordon danced,

Gordon changed in their perception forever.

As Gordon danced,

He changed on this highest spiritual level available to any human.

As Gordon danced,

He sweated.

As Gordon sweated,

He did an impressive slut drop.

GORDON *slut drops.*

MANPUSSY: At the base of Gordon's slut drop the universe gave him a gift.

A little bulge at the top of Cumpig's sock.

GORDON *takes out the baggie.*

GORDON: Oh my fucking god.

MANPUSSY: Gordon knew exactly what the drugs were because…

CUMPIG: Because I write it on the baggie with a marker pen so I know exactly what it is when I'm cunted.

MANPUSSY: And he knew exactly how to take them…

GORDON: Because I watched a documentary about Crystal Meth on the BFI player.

MANPUSSY: But Gordon hasn't tried coke let alone methamphetamine.

GORDON: No, but I do have a lot of flexi.

MANPUSSY: You've got flexi time so you'll get fucked up on Crystal Meth?

GORDON: Yes.

MANPUSSY: But you normally match all your drinks with a glass of water.

GORDON: Oh yeah, you're right, I forgot, I'm Gordon.

MANPUSSY: Gordon puts the meth inside a paracetamol packet and puts it under a toilet roll.

Like it will jump inside him or something.

He goes to his room,

Lies on the bed,

And exhausted by everything that had happened that day, falls asleep.

As he sleeps, Cumpig's email is forwarded six hundred times internally and externally at Scot Gov.

As he sleeps, he continues to make seismic shifts in the spiritual dimension.

At 7am, he wakes, and picks up his phone.

He's not heard all the messages come in because of Techno Bunker.

GORDON: Alexa stop.

Alexa doesn't stop. The tunes stay loud and twisted.

GORDON: What the fuck are all these messages?

Maybe there's been a restructure announcement?

News of a second referendum?

GORDON *screams.*

MANPUSSY: Or maybe all Gordon's colleagues had found out he set up an ass buffet at Malmaison that no one had dined at.

'You ok, hun?'

'Call me if you need anything.'

'What's going on?'

'Is this a joke?'

It wasn't a joke it was/

GORDON: Oh my God I'm Pig Gordon!

And I'm going to be fired... cancelled... redeployed... on the front of the Daily Record.

MANPUSSY: Then he found an email from his line manager, Angela,

'Gordon, hope you're ok?'

'Listen, work from home tomorrow and put some time in my diary for Monday.'

GORDON: No... wait... it wasn't me!

MANPUSSY: There were only two Gordon's in the legal team,

The other one was nearing retirement and had a cast iron alibi.

GORDON: Ok, it was me. I think I had a psychotic break. I'm back now – hi!

MANPUSSY:	The appropriation of queer culture at Scot Gov had been fierce and rapid.
	Gordon had not been part of the new obsession with LGBTQ history month or the establishment of the long running Microsoft Teams Drag Race channel.
	Gordon had never knowingly said 'yas queen'.
	No one knew the journey he'd been on with pig culture that the working group had prompted.
	And no one knew the dark place he found himself in today…that day… what we would call yesterday.
	Initially it was dark.
	Suddenly he was back on the bed in Malmaison again,
	Offering his hole to eight pig whores and 250 lawyers.
	And at first he thought –
GORDON:	Oh my god everyone knows who I really am.
	My life is over.
MANPUSSY:	But quickly he changed the narrative.
	(Beat.)
	He changed the narrative.
GORDON:	Oh my god I've done it.
	I'm a real mess.
	I'm even more of a mess than Frank from Fiscal Sustainability.
	Oh my god I'm not Gordon anymore!
MANPUSSY:	Without thinking Gordon ran to his computer printer/
GORDON:	But…
MANPUSSY:	Without thinking.

GORDON:	I've got syringes I use to fill my printer cartridges with ink.
MANPUSSY:	Who does that?
GORDON:	Me, I'm classic ESTJ.
MANPUSSY:	Gordon ran to the bathroom and recovered the Tina.
	He ran to his room and got on his sad little bed.
GORDON:	It's a king size actually, with a natural latex topper.
MANPUSSY:	He got on his lonely bed like a posh Renton and/
GORDON:	I'm not posh, I'm Pig Gordon.
	I'm a cock hungry bottom and I'm gonna be even more of a mess than Frank!
MANPUSSY:	And with that Gordon dissolved the tiniest amount of Tina in a glass of San Pellegrino, sucked it up in a spike-less syringe and skooshed it up his arse.
	Meanwhile, across town, Cumpig was opening up the gym.
	Lifting the big shutters to a soundtrack of Kylie,
	Like he always does when the bros haven't turned up yet.
	He's dancing to Kylie in his jockstrap.
CUMPIG:	Chillout Manpussy.
MANPUSSY:	Oh come on, it's sweet.
	Enjoy yourself.
	Cumpig wasn't the brains of Scotland, but he had a heart of gold and was a great little mover.
	He could squat 200 kilos like he was bouncing on a space hopper.
CUMPIG:	220.

MANPUSSY:	Haven't got that for a while though, have you?
CUMPIG:	No, have I fuck.
MANPUSSY:	Cumpig was dancing and singing out of tune over the music when/
CUMPIG:	Gordon?
	Fuck, I nearly shat myself.
GORDON:	Hi.
	It's Pig Gordon actually.
	I put drugs up my bum.
CUMPIG:	What the fuck are you wearing?
MANPUSSY:	Gordon's shorts were so tight you could almost see the drugs he put in his bum.
	And his t-shirt was cropped above the nipple.
CUMPIG:	How much did you take?
GORDON:	Just a tiny bit.
	I'm a bit of a pussy.
	On the subject of which, would you like to taste mine?
CUMPIG:	Your pussy?
GORDON:	Yes.
	Everything suddenly makes sense, Cumpig.
CUMPIG:	Except you?
GORDON:	Europe needs me.
	Us.
	People like me.
	No, actual me.
CUMPIG:	Are you ok?

GORDON: No, I'm a total fucking mess.

Want to fuck me?

CUMPIG: Aye, totally,

But Manpussy and I have this rule.

MANPUSSY: Gordon strips to a jockstrap.

He's thirsty.

GORDON: What's the rule?

Am I breaking it?

CUMPIG: No.

Sex is fine.

But I'm not allowed drugs without Manpussy.

GORDON: Well…

How were you to know my butt was full of chems when you tongued it?

CUMPIG: Fair point.

GORDON *seduces* **CUMPIG**, *running away from him.* **CUMPIG** *chases him around the gym/dancefloor.*

CUMPIG: Come here you wee bastard.

CUMPIG *captures him.*

MANPUSSY: They say there are seven stories in the world,

And that even those seven stories aren't that many.

But those stories are for straight people.

Gays get two.

They get Grease.

And Grease 2.

And Pretty Woman.

Basically any Cinderella story.

Like Brokeback Mountain.

How Brokeback Mountain?

Well… Jack Twist is Cinderella, trying to get his handsome back.

But he can't.

Because the film is made by straight people.

So he has to live in misery and then gets put to death.

Like Jesus.

Who was also Cinderella adjacent.

Anyway, we play this transient role.

We come out.

We change.

We go to the ball.

And just when we think we've found it all, we lose it.

And we're running around,

fucked off our tits,

trying to get someone to wear slippers with us.

But it's a catch-22.

Because no one wants to wear slippers with a whore.

But perhaps Gordon is different.

Perhaps he can break free.

After all, he has managed to get…

GORDON *becomes a modern art sculpture.*

CUMPIG: Both of his hands inside his own asshole!

GORDON: I'm like a Munch painting!

CUMPIG: I can't see it.

GORDON: No?

CUMPIG: Oh yeah, now I see it.

GORDON *changes position.*

GORDON: Now I'm a/

CUMPIG: Picasso?

GORDON *changes position.*

GORDON: And now?

CUMPIG: Sorry.

GORDON: Louise Bourgeois!

GORDON *changes position.*

CUMPIG: Warhol!

CUMPIG and **GORDON** *lie post-coitally on the floor of the gym.*

GORDON: Where's Manpussy?

CUMPIG: He's at home watching true crime and eating southern food.

GORDON: Doesn't he have to work?

MANPUSSY: This is my work.

I have an Etsy shop.

I've just had an idea for a line of items for it, inspired by serial killers and Gothic New England toile.

It's gonna be called Psycho cushions Qu'est-ce que gay!

GORDON: I might take a tiny bit more/

GORDON *takes the Tina out of his pocket. He holds it up.*

CUMPIG:	Gordon, no!
	Do me a favour and put it in the safe.
GORDON:	What safe?
CUMPIG:	Over there.
	Put it in the safe before I turn into a pumpkin.
GORDON:	How does that work?
CUMPIG:	Ever since SNAX last year,
	Manpussy made me promise to only take drugs with him.
	If I break the rule I have to wear orange and I can only go out annually.
GORDON:	Oh I see, like a Halloween pumpkin?
CUMPIG:	Yes, now put it in the fucking safe!
GORDON:	Where I did the Angel of the North?
CUMPIG:	Yes.

GORDON *goes to the safe.*

CUMPIG:	Set a code.
GORDON:	Done. The code is/
CUMPIG:	Don't tell me!
GORDON:	Sorry.
CUMPIG:	Put it in your phone.
GORDON:	Done.

GORDON *notices the time on his phone.*

GORDON:	Oh my fucking god, look at the time, I have to pack.
CUMPIG:	Where are you going?
GORDON:	Berlin.

CUMPIG: Oh nice, are you going for work?

GORDON: No, Cumpig, I'm going to SNAX.

CUMPIG *laughs.* **GORDON** *doesn't.*

CUMPIG: Wait, are you serious?

GORDON: Yes.

CUMPIG: You can't go to SNAX.

GORDON: Why not?

You saw my Jackson Pollock.

CUMPIG: Gordon, you're not ready.

GORDON: I'm as ready as I'll ever be.

CUMPIG: You're really not.

And by the time you reach Berlin, the Tina will wear off and you'll be spooning in the IBIS by midnight.

Go next year.

We'll plan it.

We'll go together.

GORDON: We might not be able to go to Europe next year.

We're heading towards the right-wing-ification of fascist Britain.

We'll probably be having staycations and doing compulsory Morris Dancing.

CUMPIG: They'll never make us do Morris Dancing in Scotland.

(Beat.)

Will they?

GORDON: They might.

	And Cumpig, this might sound crazy to you but I've realised who I really am.
CUMPIG:	I know what this is.
	I've seen it so many times.
	You think the real you is a fuck hole.
	But you're more than that.
	You're Gordon.
GORDON:	No, I'm not, I'm…
	I'm the European Union.
CUMPIG:	What?
GORDON:	I'm the Neue Europäische Union
	People…
	Well men..
	Men will come together as one in my body.
CUMPIG:	Ok, but can they do that next year?
GORDON:	No and my Uber is here.
	Driver, take me home,
	Take me up the bum,
	And then take me to the airport!
CUMPIG:	Gordon, wait, you've left/
MANPUSSY:	Gordon had left his report again.
	Cumpig chased after his Uber but they didn't see him.
	Cumpig got his phone out to email Gordon and found an automatic response from…
CUMPIG:	The Scottish Government legal team group mailbox?

MANPUSSY:	Addicts manipulate any situation to get what they want.
CUMPIG:	It's not that.
	I'm not addict.
	Oh fuck!
MANPUSSY:	Every situation.
CUMPIG:	I'm not an addict, I'm an arsehole.
MANPUSSY:	Meanwhile at mine and Cumpig's flat,
	I've watched all of the Avenger films.
	Spent some time revisiting Dawson's Creek.
	Skyped my parents.
	Skyped Cumpig's grandmother.
	And now I'm lying on the chez longe wondering if I will ever write a novel.
	Thinking that I can't be fucked actually.
	But perhaps some performance poetry when,
	Cumpig walks in, what the fuck?
CUMPIG:	Oh my god Tom, I've outed that boy Gordon at his work,
	So he's taken some Tina he found in my sock,
	And now he's off to SNAX to become a pig whore and he thinks he's the New European Union.
MANPUSSY:	That makes no sense.
CUMPIG:	It does to him.
	He's crazy.
	I have to go and look after him.

MANPUSSY:	Do you think I'm stupid?
CUMPIG:	No, I'm the stupid one.
MANPUSSY:	After what happened last year, if you think I'm going back there because of some privileged, deluded hot mess you've just met you can think again.
CUMPIG:	I'm in love with him.
MANPUSSY:	Shit.
CUMPIG:	I know.
MANPUSSY:	Are you sure?
CUMPIG:	Yes.
MANPUSSY:	*(To us.)* Cumpig falls in love fast, but this speed is unprecedented.
CUMPIG:	*(To us.)* Love. Real love with someone pure of heart, gives me something to obsess about that's not drugs or alcohol.
MANPUSSY:	Don't manipulate them, that's my job.
CUMPIG:	I'll be there for you.
Beat.	
MANPUSSY:	'I'll be there for you.'
	It was our only wedding vow so he knew it could be quite emotive.
CUMPIG:	We're all one.
MANPUSSY:	Are you high?
CUMPIG:	No.
MANPUSSY:	Show me your pupils.
CUMPIG:	I maybe got some Tina off him when I rimmed on the incline bench.
MANPUSSY:	Is Gordon worth turning into a pumpkin for?

CUMPIG: I think he maybe is.

MANPUSSY: Well that's your costume sorted,

What the fuck am I gonna wear?

CUMPIG: Yas!

MANPUSSY: Meanwhile, Gordon was at the airport.

Ahead of him, at the check-in, was a big group of gays.

All happy, and laughing and joking together.

One of the group noticed him and smiled.

Gordon didn't smile back because he felt really self-conscious in his outfit.

Which maybe wasn't a bad thing.

He looked a bit like he'd been in a traffic accident,

and had to be cut out of his clothes.

He went to the toilets and saw himself in the mirror.

GORDON: Who the fuck am I?

MANPUSSY: He thought.

He was crashing.

He quickly changed into preppy, boring clothes,

Put his party outfit in his wee case,

And made his way back outside to the airport bus.

As the bus pulled up/

GORDON: Cumpig!

Manpussy!

I forgot something.

CUMPIG: What did you forget?

GORDON:	I'm Gordon.
MANPUSSY:	Gordon went to get on the bus.
	Cumpig grabbed him and pulled him in to his bright orange sportswear,
	Kissing him,
	Shoving a hand down Gordon's trousers,
	And thrusting a finger up his bum.
	The smoothest airport drugs handover ever.
GORDON:	Drugs?
MANPUSSY:	Oh Gordon, please.
	We stumble through security and Gordon enjoys a quick frisk from Patricia – here to help you and keep you safe.
	He enjoys it a bit too much.
	Gordon!
	In the departure lounge, our flight is boarding.
	Last call!
	Last call!
	Cumpig, get a litre of vodka from duty free!
CUMPIG:	It's the last call!
	Do you want some salt and vinegar Discos?
MANPUSSY:	Yes!
	And a litre of vodka and hold the flight!
CUMPIG:	Ok!
MANPUSSY:	I normally need a six-week lead time for a SNAX outfit.
	I like to say something political.

Ideally, this time, I'd wear something about the cost of living crisis with real diamonds, but there's no time.

I'm going to have to get my outfit from duty free.

Which is quite limiting.

Then inspiration hits…

Since early 2020 I've been learning Riverdance online.

I'm now in the top 10% in Scotland and the top 23% globally.

I have my Irish jig shoes in a bag because I practice everywhere.

I pick up some key pieces and a copy of Vogue.

CUMPIG: Manpussy!

MANPUSSY: Coming!

On the flight, Gordon and Cumpig are practically fucking in the seats next to me.

I'm in the aisle seat so I can practice the steps.

Well half of the steps with one foot but they're the same on both sides.

I listen to 'Lord of the Dance' on repeat.

Gordon steals the life jacket from under my seat.

GORDON *puts on an a life jacket.*

GORDON: I've always wanted one.

Why did you come and rescue me, Cumpig?

CUMPIG: Because you're pure of heart.

GORDON: I'm not.

CUMPIG: You are.

You didn't let on that I outed you at your work.

GORDON:	I didn't want you to feel bad.
CUMPIG:	I know, you're nice.
MANPUSSY:	I take my seatbelt off and stand up, practising some of the bigger Lord of the Dance moves with both feet, and affording Gordon enough time to pop the end of Cumpig's penis between his lips.
	We land in Berlin, but I'm still flying.
	For the pre-club, we go to Bull where I found out who I was in 2016.
	In Bull Gordon notices:
GORDON:	Is that man sucking piss out of that other man's nappy?
MANPUSSY:	Yes, Gordon.
	Yes, he is.
GORDON:	Cumpig was right, I'm not ready for this.
MANPUSSY:	Gordon turns to flee but then this cute you guy catches his eye.
CUMPIG:	*(As Olek.)* What's your name?
	Hi, I'm Olek, what are you called?
GORDON:	Hi, Olek, I'm Gordon.
CUMPIG:	*(As Olek.)* Where are you from, Gordon?
GORDON:	I'm from Scotland.
CUMPIG:	*(As Olek.)* Oh nice, with the skirts?
	Did you bring it?
GORDON:	Oh, you mean the kilt.
	No, I came with hand luggage only.
	Sorry, my chat sucks, Olek.

CUMPIG:	*(As Olek.)* I mean it is entry level chat but you're fine.
	Relax.
GORDON:	Oh my god, I am so sorry.
MANPUSSY:	Olek laughs.
CUMPIG:	*(As Olek.)* Don't be sorry.
	Just be yourself.
GORDON:	I don't know who that is.
CUMPIG:	*(As Olek.)* Nobody does.
GORDON:	Oh my god you don't need this.
CUMPIG:	*(As Olek.)* Oh fuck off Gordon.
	Nobody really knows who they are.
	It's a lifelong adventure.
	Now stick out your tongue.
MANPUSSY:	Olek bites a pill in half, puts it on Gordon's tongue and disappears into the dark room.
	Gordon follows him.
	Gordon, you better not be giving Olek any more shit chat!
CUMPIG:	*(As Olek.)* No, he's being hilarious.
	Listen to this.
GRODON:	I'm the New EU!
CUMPIG:	*(As Olek.)* Oh yeah? Can I cum inside you?
GORDON:	Yeah!
CUMPIG:	*(As Olek.)* Yeah?
GORDON:	Yes!
MANPUSSY:	Gordon emerges from the dark room.

Olek follows clutching one of Gordon's slip-on loafers.

Gordon makes an announcement to Bull.

Friends, Romans, Countrymen,

I don't know who I am, and neither do any of you, and I'm going to SNAX.

And then he's out the door.

Me and Cumpig and Olek grab our stuff and go after him.

I pull them into a doorway for a quick team talk.

I put on my teacher voice.

Eyeballing each of them.

Tonight no G.

Got it?

CUMPIG:	*(As Olek.)* I'm having G.
MANPUSSY:	Says Olek.
	You can do as you please.
	But Cumpig, no G or you know what will happen?
CUMPIG:	No G.
MANPUSSY:	If you do G, I do scat.
GORDON:	Oh my god, will people really be doing scat?
MANPUSSY:	I will be, Gordon, if Cumpig takes G.
	Got it?
GORDON:	Got it.
CUMPIG:	Got it.
MANPUSSY:	Then we walk to the U-Bahn.
	We're silent and in slow motion

And we're probably in black and white too.

An old woman passes me, my jacket flaps open and she notices my outfit.

She smiles.

Welcome to Europe.

We pass the Berlin wall.

I think about how quickly things can change when they change.

How you wait around for ages and nothing happens and then suddenly David Hasselof is on top of you singing,

And everyone wants a piece of you.

How borders that seem immovable can be torn down.

That sometimes that's good and sometimes that's bad.

That Berlin knows this better than anyone.

We get off the U-bhan at Warschauer Straße,

And walk through the waste ground leading to Berghain.

With one hand in Cumpig's and one hand in Olek's.

Gordon realises:

GORDON: Oh my god, there are lots of different parts of me.

Parts of me are boring like Edinburgh.

Parts of me are romantic like Barcelona.

Parts of me are gritty like Marseille.

Parts of me are mad and you can only go to them for the weekend like Newcastle.

Parts of me are sexual and have red lights like London.

Parts of me have big latex cocks in the windows like Amsterdam.

Parts of me like honey waffles and hot chocolates like… IKEA.

Parts of me likes drinking all-inclusive drinks and eating sausage beans and chips on a Spanish Island.

Parts of me are cinematic like Warsaw.

Parts of me are dramatic like Prague.

Parts of me are a like spunk on a t-shirt in Benidorm.

There are lots of parts of me.

And this is just one.

I am the European Union.

MANPUSSY: Gordon didn't just think any of that he said it all, loudly,

To everyone in the queue at Berghain.

And then it happens.

The pipes and the drums begin in my head,

And I charge my legs with energy,

Ready to perform the sacred moves.

Ireland is still in the Europe Union.

Whenever I Riverdance I'm in Ireland.

I look East and the Molecule Men are wrestling or fighting or fucking or whatever they're doing.

And then I look West and I see the moon,

And the moon has the face of Jean Butler.

And she says 'now!'.

'Now Manpussy!'

'Now!'

MANPUSSY *Riverdances.*

They all Riverdance with him.

MANPUSSY *leaps. He comes crashing down.*

MANPUSSY *holds up the butt plug microphone to his lips.*

MANPUSSY:	'Nicht heute. Entschuldigung. Du musst in Sportbekleidung sein,' says Sven.
GORDON:	Sven is the legendary Berghain doorman.
	Tattoos all over/
MANPUSSY:	Gordon, you're not even here.
	You've gone inside with Cumpig and Olek already.
	(To us.) Gordon had lifted his shirt and flashed his sportswear and sailed through.
GORDON:	Oh my god I'm inside!
	I'm in Berghain!

GORDON *and* **CUMPIG** *rush into the club.*

MANPUSSY:	'Not tonight, sorry, you must wear sportswear only.'
	Sven repeats to me in English.
	I can't breathe.
	I'm supposed to style it out and walk away.
	But I gasp for air.
	My husband is in there, I whimper.
	'Then he's everyone's husband now.'
	You don't understand.
	Last time we were here his heart stopped beating.
	I had to punch him in the chest to start it again.

He doesn't have any control.

I'm his control!

I'm his control!

'Nicht Heute. Du musst in Sportbekleidung sein.'

GORDON: *(To us.)* Then me and Cumpig/

MANPUSSY: What are you doing?

GORDON: I'm narrating.

MANPUSSY: Why?

GORDON: Because you didn't get in.

MANPUSSY: But I'm narrating because I didn't get in.

Oh my god, I'm not here, am I?

GORDON: Sorry, Manpussy.

We looked for you but we were so high we forgot
and…

MANPUSSY: I'm just having an existential crisis in the Lidl carpark,
amn't I?

GORDON: Probably.

MANPUSSY: Fuck!

MANPUSSY *moves towards the upstage exit.*

MANPUSSY: And then I see them…

Hanging in the branches of a tree in the Lidl carpark.

A pair of swimming trunks.

They've seen better days.

Someone's soiled them and thrown there to dry in the
sun,

But they're technically sportswear.

MANPUSSY *exits the space completely.*

GORDON: We're in this big bright changing area.

I'm holding a transparent bin bag they gave me on the door and I…

GORDON *undresses and puts his clothes in the bag and gets into his sportswear.*

He holds up the bag.

GORDON: This… this is Gordon.

CUMPIG: *(As Olek.)* Stop thinking, Gordon and enjoy yourself.

GORDON: I don't exist.

CUMPIG: *(As Olek.)* No, no one does.

GORDON: Hume was right.

CUMPIG: *(As Olek.)* Of course he was right.

GORDON: I'm not here to bring all men together, I'm here because I'm a privileged cunt with a passport.

CUMPIG: *(As Olek.)* If you think so…

You can chose whatever narrative works for you.

If you want to sing out, sing out.

If you want to be free, be free.

GORDON: And with that, Olek dances into Berghain like a god.

And Cumpig takes my hand.

I look at him and dive into his eyes,

Those deep pools.

He grips my hand and we walk towards the wall of sound.

I can feel every molecule in my body.

I don't exist.

I never have.

We pass lots of people fucking and they're not other.

They're all part of me.

We're all one.

I don't even speak.

CUMPIG: You do, but it's cute.

GORDON: Me an Cumpig rise up the staircase and go into the turbine hall.

Just as Boris is starting his set.

And then we dance.

And I can fucking dance.

CUMPIG: You can fucking dance, Gordon.

GORDON: So can Cumpig.

CUMPIG: Oh aye.

GORDON: But then I notice this guy and he notices me.

And I try to hide form him and his Prince Charming energy.

I try to dance away from his gaze.

But I can't.

CUMPIG: What's wrong?

GORDON: Nothing, I lie to Cumpig.

But I lose all sense of rhythm.

Cumpig notices it.

He throws his arms around me.

I hold him and shut my eyes, wanting Prince Charming to disappear.

But when I open my eyes he's there.

And he takes me from Cumpig.

Cumpig dances away from us.

And Prince Charming turns me around and holds me.

And he kisses the back of my neck.

I'm Gordon again, aren't I?

I say it out loud.

Hi Gordon, I'm Fabian, he whispers and he licks my ear.

I can't take my eyes off Cumpig.

No one can.

Everyone loves him.

Of course they do.

CUMPIG: No thanks, mate.

GORDON: Says Cumpig, to a cute guy offering a pipette.

CUMPIG: No G for me.

GORDON: He says, but it's totally unconvincing.

I want to take the pipette, lock it in a safe and throw away the key.

But Prince Charming is…

Wait a minute…

What the fuck?

Are you spooning me?

'Yeah man', he says, 'do you like it?'

And I see Olek across the dance floor, practically flying.

If you want to be free, be free!

'Eh?', he says, licking the sweat from my neck.

I push him off me and I shout – Prince Charming can go and fuck himself and I'm gonna watch the bitch!

And I dance towards Cumpig.

Making shapes that baffle his wee group of muscled fans.

I use every move my body can make to tempt him away from the G.

And it seems to be working.

I distract him but I'm gonna need back up.

MANPUSSY *enters wearing a magical costume fashioned from swimming trunks and a lifejacket.*

MANPUSSY:	Ich habe einen Schokoladenkuchen in meiner Unterhose germacht!
CUMPIG:	What?
MANPUSSY:	I have made a chocolate cake in my pants!
GORDON:	Says Manpussy as he turns Cumpig into a pumpkin.

CUMPIG *turns into a pumpkin.*

MANPUSSY *pulls the toggle on his lifejacket and it inflates, and suddenly rising over the funky, perverted techno is the triumphant chorus of 'Ode to Joy'.*

MANPUSSY *lip-syncs to it. On the final note of the song, that* **MANPUSSY** *holds for absolutely ages,* **MANPUSSY**, **GORDON** *and* **CUMPIG** *have an ecstatic chocolate cake food fight.*

CUMPIG:	What the fuck are you wearing?
MANPUSSY:	Sportswear.
CUMPIG:	Really?
	What sport is this?

MANPUSSY:	The concept is actually subversive wild swimming.
	Or subversive submersion as I told the door staff.
GORDON:	Reunited in Berghain and about to go and get fucked sideways by every cunt in the place,
	I realised what I wanted wasn't a Prince Charming,
	It wasn't even anonymous loads,
	Even though I'm totally up for that.
	I wanted a Cumpig or a Manpussy.
CUMPIG:	You can have us whenever you like, babes.
MANPUSSY:	He means of his own.
	You mean you want your own Cumpig or Manpussy?
GORDON:	Yes, I want a soul mate.
	I want the other part of me that's not boring,
	But loves me and will go on adventures with me.
MANPUSSY:	You're destroying me.
	Well done, I'm dead inside.
	Let's go.
GORDON:	But I'm covered in… chocolate cake?
MANPUSSY:	Let's say that.
GORDON:	And I have no pants on.
	And I'm drenched in other people's piss.
	And Berghain is so much.
	The energy is….
MANPUSSY:	Come on!
CUMPIG:	We go through to the labyrinth.

	And I'm proud.
	I'm proud of myself and I'm proud of my friends.
GORDON:	In the big room of fucking you can hardly see twenty feet in front of you for all the banging of arseholes.
	Manpussy continues the swimming theme and dives into a sea of bodies.
MANPUSSY:	You can try and make it sound pretty if you like, lovely,
	But I basically swallow about fifty dicks.
	And take fifteen loads.
	But if you want to sound pretty.
	Why don't we say,
	That I lie like Thomas Chatterton,
	Draped across men from all over the world,
	Whilst someone feeds me the semen that/
GORDON:	Cumpig finds a prime spot.
	The cigarette smoke catches the light filtering through it.
	Manpussy is a few metres back,
	Taking it from two guys.
MANPUSSY:	Four.
GORDON:	Four.
	He notices me noticing him.
	He smiles at me.
	He beams.
	And me of yore would be with Prince Charming,

In a budding co-dependent relationship.

Wondering if we'll ever own a flat in the Barbican together.

But not anymore.

I am Gordon.

I am a vortex to the New European Union.

In the interest of taste and decency I won't go into too much detail of the next forty-eight hours.

At a physical level I am a dumping ground.

An anteroom.

A host.

But spiritually I am soaring through the universe.

I am taking us somewhere we've never been before.

I'm taking us somewhere new.

The music stops.

GORDON: Back in Edinburgh on the Monday night we get off the number 100 at Waverley Bridge and reality hits me like…

MANPUSSY: Like reality.

You can't get worse than that.

GORDON: I look up at the Scott Monument,

That looks like a giant gothic knob directing us all to heaven,

And I realise that I probably won't see Cumpig and Manpussy again in my life.

CUMPIG: Fuck off, you will.

MANPUSSY: Not this week.

But you will, of course you will.

GORDON: Shall we go for one last drink?

CUMPIG: No, fuck that.

I'm done.

And Gordon, I love you.

I do.

But I'm shite at goodbyes.

And I need to lie down in a darkened room.

GORDON *grabs* **CUMPIG** *and holds him.* **GORDON** *cries.*

CUMPIG: And Gordon holds me in his posh, arms and I could stay in them forever but – bye!

GORDON: As I hit Princes Street I put my shades and tunes on

And thank fuck the trams go in slow motion or I would have got squashed.

I find myself at the bar in Planet and some big handsome walks up to me and thinks I'm boring.

'Want to spoon me?' he says,

I smile and shake my head.

Sorry, I only like raw, anonymous kink.

He looks confused and walks away.

A week later I say hello on our WhatsApp group.

We said we'd remind each other to get tested.

I came off the worst: chlamydia and gonorrhoea, but the prep kept me negative.

Cumpig had gonorrhea in the throat and up the arse.

Manpussy had chlamydia.

MANPUSSY: Actually I was fine.

I just said that for solidarity.

GORDON: And that was the last I heard of them.

Until 2029.

I messaged the group.

On the off chance, they were in Berlin.

Like I was.

With my partner in crime Big Stevie.

Big Stevie and I were kind of over parties like SNAX,

But we wanted to go to dance and to reminisce…

We'd both been there in 2022.

Arriving was fun.

To celebrate Scotland voting Yes, becoming an independent country again and re-joining the EU,

There was piper piping us into Berghain.

It was funny and cute.

I felt like a tiny part of it.

Because at work I'd helped to write the legislation that made it possible for Scotland to get a second referendum.

Oh I'd kept my job.

My line manager Angela said I needed to maintain my work life divide but I think she was secretly proud of me.

And I got together with an insatiable fuck buddy from the mailroom.

Who in turn introduced me to Big Stevie at a party in the Travelodge.

As they piped us into Berghain,

The drone of the bagpipes melding with the Funktion-One sound system,

Went through my bones and I got a wee tear in my eye.

There's no phones in Berghain,

Said big Stevie.

Oh shit, yes.

I was turning mine off when/

CUMPIG *puts his hand in the air. He's pumping his hands to the music.*

GORDON: I get a hands in the air from Cumpig.

CUMPIG: From Marcus.

MANPUSSY *puts his hands in the air too. He pumps his hands.*

GORDON: And a wink face tongue out from Manpussy.

MANPUSSY: From Tom.

They dance together.

GORDON: We dance together.

                   They haven't changed.

CUMPIG: We're sober.

GORDON: Are you?

CUMPIG: Are we fuck.

                   But we do harm reduction classes.

GORDON: Do you?

CUMPIG: Sometimes.

GORDON: We don't have anything to say to each other, but it
                   doesn't matter.

MANPUSSY:	Does it fuck.
	It's just nice to see you.
GORDON:	Yes.
CUMPIG:	Big Stevie looks nice.
GORDON:	Big Stevie is nice.
	I cuddle him.
CUMPIG:	Enjoy yourselves.
GORDON:	And then my husband takes me from the dancefloor.
	And we find a quiet place.
	A dumping ground.
	It looks and smells familiar.
	And I look around to check we're alone.
	And I do something super perverted.
	Alone.
	With my husband.
	In the centre of the new Europe.

Blackout.

Washed

New!

Washed
New!

**A True
Story**

S A N D R A   B O Y D

Carpenter's Son Publishing

Washed New!

©2021

Published by Carpenter's Son Publishing, Franklin, TN.

Edit and Interior Design by Adept Content Solutions

Printed in the United States of America

ISBN 978-1-952025-51-8

CONTENTS

PREFACE

My best friend told me that she wanted to go see Dr. Cindy Trimm, and I said sure even though I had never heard of Dr. Trimm. I had no idea how impactful this would be in my life. The closer we got to the days of the event, things started going wrong. I started to be attacked in a spiritual sense and suddenly had many disagreements with people; I wondered what was going on. We pressed on and flew to Atlanta to attend Dr. Cindy Trimm's End of Year conference in December 2018. During one of the altar calls, a pastor put his hands on my head, and I fell to the ground, which was a first for me. I got up, and I was not the same. I felt it. It had been a long time since a powerful preacher and leader had given me encouragement and described the steps I needed to take to move forward with my calling.

I want this book to encourage and give you hope. God gave me love and an opportunity to get it right again. He has washed me new, and since He did it for me, He can do it for you too. Come join me as I share my life story and testimonies. It's October 2020, and I have learned so much about myself and who I am becoming. I could not have made it without God, so I want to share with you how having faith, sowing seeds, repenting, and surrendering can lead you to an unimagined new you. Being in the presence of God can touch and transform your life. Imagine praying and having your prayers answered right there.

Being in the presence of God can touch and transform your life.

ACKNOWLEDGMENTS

So many people have played a part in my life, and I want to thank them all.

Anna, Cesar, and Kristine, you have been so unconditionally loving to me. Your friendship has taught me so much. Thank you all for having been there in both my good times and bad. I will never forget it.

Ann, Griselda, Myrna, and Francis, I am so grateful for all your love and for your friendship. You loved me even at my weakest.

To Yvette and Joshua, thank you for being in my life and for loving me the way you do. You give me a reason to press on.

INTRODUCTION

Have you ever asked yourself what your God-given purpose was? I asked myself the same question, and I started asking God to reveal my purpose to me.

In 2013, I was at my lowest point emotionally. I had separated from my husband. There were days when I did not even want to get out of bed or get out of my pajamas because I was hurting so much. I felt depressed and hopeless. On top of the emotional stress of my broken marriage, I was uncertain of my financial stability. My children were three and five years old and would stay with me most of the time during the school year; during the summers, my husband and I split the time. I was filled with uncertainty about my life's path and the fear of not knowing if I would be able to maintain my home on one income and keep a roof over my kids' heads. I did not know if I would have enough to feed them and give them the same comfort that they were used to.

I felt guilty because I was choosing to give up on my marriage. I knew firsthand the pain of abandonment because

I had experienced it when my own father left me when I was seven years old. I had sworn to myself that no matter what, I would never divorce because I wanted to prevent that brokenness that I had experienced in my kids' lives.

I was familiar with the pain of divorce because I had seen my poor, frail mother deal with the consequences of one. All my life, I had struggled with not knowing what it felt like to be wanted and loved. This caused me to go through depression and anger, mostly a rage against my father. Here I was about to break the covenant of marriage, and instead of taking ownership for my faults, I went to God to complain about my husband. Here I was blaming the demise of the marriage on my husband when in reality it was both of us.

The one right thing I did when my life was crumbling down was pray and seek God. I prayed fervently, and one day I asked God what he wanted me to do. A local pastor told me that God wanted me to write a book. She said that this book would be like pancakes; there would never be enough on the shelves because it would be a best seller. Even though she said that, I tried to escape my divine mission like Jonah did in the Bible. I did not obey at that moment because I was bitter about my painful divorce.

The idea of writing a book meant that I had to relive the pain, and I was not ready for that.

I thought, *Lord, You don't want me to talk about how angry and hurt I am right now.* I carried on with my life. I promised in my heart to God that the book would be done by December 31, 2018. I had been taking notes here and there, but I was not focused. I always spoke of it. All my friends and coworkers were tired of hearing me talk about a book that I never delivered. Even I was tired of just talking about it, but I excused myself by thinking, It happened to me so it will be easy to do it once I decide to. Well, it was not easy. A book will not write itself; my prophetic word needed activation. I was holding on to everything inside when God wanted me to release it to help someone else be set free.

I prayed fervently, and one day I asked God what he wanted me to do.

One day, all at once the front tires of my car started wobbling. I thought it was a tire issue, but it turned out the front axle in my old Lexus needed to be replaced. That cost a pretty penny. Then my home air conditioner stopped working. The Florida heat is unbearable at times, and for days, I had no air conditioner. Then my dishwasher went dead, and my freezer stopped working. My heart started palpitating so severely that I could not bear the pain. It was December 31, 2018, and I knew why this was happening to me. I had promised God, and again I had failed him. I repented and went straight to the hospital with my kids. I had a blue dye test done to see if I had any blood clots. The doctor said I had a had a healthy heart but that I needed to have less stress in my life along with living a healthier lifestyle. My kids and I were there in the hospital room long enough to watch the New Year's Eve ball drop.

In January 2019, I called a publishing company and signed a contract to publish my book. This was an act of faith on my part because I had to start paying money for something that was not even written. Aligning myself with my destiny, I started to write and put into words all that had happened to me. This book is about my shattered life and testimonies. I share what I learned by being obedient and what happened to me when I was being rebellious and disobedient.

This book is my way of honoring God. Father, I love you more than my words can express. I thank You for everything that You have done in my life and for not giving me what I asked for at times. You took me from nothing to being almost complete. I am so grateful for and humbled by Your love and kindness. I have failed You so many times, and still You love me. I repent, Lord; use me for your Glory and this time I will obey. I come into alignment with my destiny right now in the mighty name of Jesus.

Chapter 1

THE NEWS OF THE ULTRASOUND

In early 2018, I went for an ultrasound because I had started bleeding vaginally when I was not on my menstrual cycle. I was worried about it, and I finally got the courage and time off work to set up a doctor's appointment to get it checked out. I was told I had an ovarian cyst that could possibly be ovarian cancer.

Normally, I am a stoic person, but at that moment, I was emotional. I started crying, and I was scared. I felt very vulnerable. I cried out, "Holy Spirit, do not leave me now." The possibility of having a problem with my ovary was not new to me. In 2004, when I was 30, I had gone through a similar situation when I was told I had to have a cyst the size of a volleyball and my ovary removed.

I was also pregnant for the first time. I was shocked and scared about my situation and was told I had to have an abortion so the cyst could be tested, or I could take my chances. The doctor told me if the cancer spread (that was if the cyst resulted in being malignant), I could die. I did not even think twice. I refused to have an abortion and decided to proceed with my pregnancy. I told God I was going to trust Him.

That same year, I had accepted Jesus Christ into my life, and my faith was immediately tested. It was easy to say that I would just trust Him, but from the moment I decided to keep both the cyst and my baby, I cried and cried. I wanted that baby more than I wanted my own life. If a choice needed to be made of whom to save, I told my husband to save the baby.

I blamed the cyst on myself as punishment for my past sins, of which I had many. As my baby grew inside of me, the cyst grew too. Months passed until the cyst burst. My husband was working overnight, so I drove my myself to the hospital in pain that felt like burning acid inside my body. I won't tell you how fast I was going so I won't get arrested for going over the speed limit. I live in a city about 45 miles from the Orlando hospital where I was supposed to have my delivery. They called my doctor in along with another surgeon. One took out the tiny baby, and the other removed the oversized ovarian cyst. My healthy baby girl was born over one month early; we named our miracle baby Yvette.

If you are wondering, "Can you have a baby with only one ovary," the answer is yes. I know because after Yvette was born, her brother, Joshua, joined our family.

In 2018, a new cyst formed on my remaining ovary, and I did not know if this cyst was cancerous or benign. If it tested cancerous, it would have to be removed. My gynecologist referred me to another specialist. I was 45 at that time, and the specialist recommended that I have a

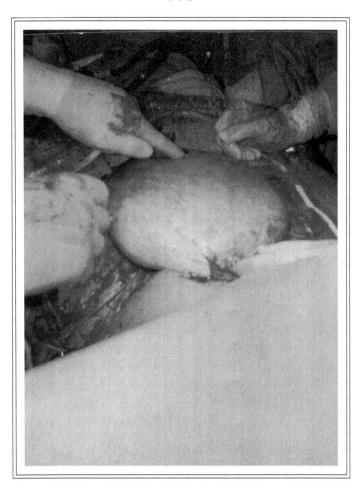

My oversized ovarian cyst

hysterectomy. I started to stress. I would no longer be able to have any more children, and I was not ready for that.

Yes, I recognized I already had my two children, but I always thought I would remarry, what if the amazing man I'd always dreamed of wanted children? If I had a hysterectomy, I would not be able to bear him a child; however, there was the risk of me being older and overweight and having a child. All those thoughts ran through my mind as I was faced with the decision. I thought, *Maybe I am overthinking it.* I decided to walk into the unknown and trust God.

I decided to walk into the unknown and trust God.

When the second cyst was discovered, my life was all about my job and children. I had a fear of not being able to see my kids go to high school, graduate from college, and grow up into adulthood in case the cyst was cancerous. I wanted to be around when they learned to drive and more. I was scared of never falling in love.

I wanted the opportunity to live life to the fullest, to go dancing in the park, to be able to get on a plane and go to Africa and Israel. I wanted to travel the world and spread the gospel. I wanted to see snow for the first time. I wanted to see the ball drop in New York City on New Year's Eve. I have a bucket list I will be checking off.

Chapter 2
MY BACKGROUND

I am originally from Pharr, Texas. I am a Mexican-American who grew up in poverty in a place called Rancho Sanchez. Growing up on a dirt road where people knew where we lived because when it rained our cars would get so muddy was humbling. We were so poor that we never had new clothes; most of our clothes were handed down or came from consignment stores. My mother did not have much, but she still wanted us to look presentable. Our home had no air conditioner, so the 90- to 100-degree weather during the Texas summers was torturous. We used to keep the box fan in the window, hoping to get a breeze inside of our rooms.

I am the daughter of a migrant worker, my mom Teresa. I come from a family of six siblings four sisters and two brothers. I am the second oldest. My nickname was "La Negra." It translates to "the black female." My mom called me that as a term of endearment because I was the darkest daughter.

When I was seven years old, my mom told my father, Gustavo, not to come by our house anymore because my stepdad would leave her because he was jealous and insecure. I don't know when my parents divorced. I know my mom was pregnant with my brother Alejandro and she hadn't even told my father about her pregnancy. My father was in the Army, and he fought in Korea.

I did not see or talk to my biological dad for more than two decades. I carried twenty-three years of brokenness and sorrow in my heart, along with hatred and rage toward my father because he walked away from us.

All I ever wanted to hear was my father saying he loved me. Year after year, I felt a growing void and pain of feeling rejected and worthless. It just kept growing and holding me in bondage. Imagine never hearing these words from your father: "Baby girl, I love you." "Happy birthday, my daughter." "I know you fell, but get up again; I've got you."

I say this because I know life experiences are not always good, but if you are the person who does not say these words to the people who love you, then I urge you to do it. Tomorrow is not guaranteed.

Maybe someone important to you has never told you they love you because they are unable to for various reasons. My father was not there when I was young, so I know firsthand how it feels to be unloved.

I understand these reasons now; however, I needed to hear those words then. I was broken and starving for these simple words which maybe would have helped me had I heard them when I was growing up. Many of us need this so we can heal and move forward. Trust me, pick up the phone, WhatsApp them, Facetime them, instant message them, text them. It does not matter how you contact them; just do it. Tell your children you love them; tell your parents you love them.

Trust me, pick up the phone, WhatsApp them, Facetime them, instant message them, text them. It does not matter how you contact them; just do it. Tell your children you love them; tell your parents you love them.

If someone has hurt you, it is time to heal and let it go. Find the person who caused that pain if you can and tell them what you feel. If it is anger or hurt, tell them. If you messed up and need to apologize, just do it. It is time to close this chapter of your life. It is time to heal and put that pain in the past. If they do not apologize or accept what you have to say, that is on them. By you letting it go, you are setting yourself free.

As of that day, you move forward. You let go of the pain by leaving it in your past. Surrender anything that is holding you back. Just give it to God; there is nothing too big for God. You just have to believe it.

At thirty years old, I finally looked for the man who had abandoned me: my father, Gustavo. I thank my ex-husband for encouraging me to do this. He told me that I was so broken and that if our marriage was going to work at all, I had to heal from my past. I hesitated at first but then listened to my ex's advice. I reached out to my sister Gladys to let the word out that I was ready to talk to my father.

If you've been in this same place, it's time to move on. I know it is hard; my tears were all over my shirt. I understand. I cried buckets when I reached out to my dad.

Chapter 3

MY MOTHER

W hy did my mom tell my dad to leave and not come back?

She told her cheating ex-husband, father of three of us, to not come back and see his kids because her new husband was untrusting and jealous. My stepdad is from Mexico. He became an American citizen after marrying my mom. He was also insecure about the presence of another man being around his wife even though my dad had only come to see his kids and not her. He told Mom he would leave her if our dad came back to see us.

My stepdad, Kiko, worked in the fields with my mom until we stopped migrating. After that he became a carpenter. He is now disabled because he had a stroke.

Back then, both he and my mom had horrible trust issues. My mom was still bitter about the betrayal of my dad, and she made life miserable at times for all of us, not just for my stepdad. Mom was emotionally broken and not spiritually developed. She had no relationship with God during our childhood. I look back and think of all the times she struggled with depression. In my family, depression is something we never spoke of because there was no money to treat it, and neither was it considered a reason to stop working.

I wish I had been wiser to be able to help her back then. Since my stepdad had no steady job or education, my mom did not respect or appreciate him. Most of the time, he would let her vent as she would yell things at him like, "*Largate* (go away)!" He was not allowed to tell us anything or correct us. She told him he could not touch us.

Imagine growing up under my mom, a broken, bitter woman who hit us with anything she found to express her frustration. She did not spare the rod. I understand the biblical meaning of "do not spare the rod," but there is a difference between physical abuse and correction. Let me try and forget that part. I will leave my past behind. I have forgiven her and myself.

When I was forty-three, my mother came to visit me in Florida. I was holding resentment toward her for our painful past, judging her and being upset at her. I was mad at her for having pushed my father away all those years ago. It was like she chose her happiness instead of ours.

What I did not know was that every time that my dad, Gustavo, had tried to visit us, my stepdad beat my mother. When she told me this, I was driving my car and she was in the passenger seat. Tears raced down my face, and I had to restrain myself because my stepdad was in the backseat. I told my mom that I was sorry and that I did not know this. She had kept it hidden from us, and maybe it was something that I had blocked out of my memory. All I know is that things appear to be better. My stepdad needs my mom as much as she needs him. My mom is now seventy years old, and I share the same birthday with my stepdad—but I always wanted my own cake, ha.

My Mother

Mom and I

Chapter 4
MIGRANT LIFE

For many years while growing up, we migrated between Texas and Naples, Florida. We went there during the school year. My mom and stepdad worked in in the fields. They had no education, so their employment options were limited. We lived either in a trailer home or in a one-room hole-in-the-wall. Imagine a family of eight crammed into one room—disgusting.

They worked at El Dudas Farm and Six Ls. I remember my mom made only pennies per bucket of tomatoes. The buckets were large, and she had to kneel, bend, and then put the basket full of tomatoes over her shoulder to hand it to the person collecting them in the truck. On holidays, my siblings and I would feel even more guilty when our mother would walk with her clothes dirty, her hands blistered, and her back in severe pain from carrying those large buckets of tomatoes on her back; my mom is only 4'11" tall. Mami (Spanish for "mom") said the field work was so torturous that every time she started working the

One bedroom where my family lived.

new season, she would vomit because of the torture and pain in her body.

Mom told me that going to school was important, so she would do whatever she had to as long as she had to so she could provide for us and let us continue our education. For years, knowing how hard my mom struggled just to feed us and put shoes on our feet made me hate my real dad even more.

Where was he? How could someone be a sperm donor and walk away from his own kids? I was angry because my mother told us he did not give us any child support. How could my birth father just walk away from my brother, sister, and me when we were still so young?

I hated him from the core of my heart. I was so hurt. Because of this insecurity, I only dated guys I knew I would never marry. I was scared to get even more hurt or disappointed. I did this for years without realizing I was hurting myself in the process. The idea of marriage was inconceivable to me at that time. I was not ready to get close to someone and set myself up to get hurt.

When I was thirteen years old, there was a twenty-one-year-old man whose family approached my mom and stepfather. He asked permission to court me so it could lead to marriage. I liked the attention the man gave me. When I would go wash clothes at the community laundry room, he would always be there to try to and talk to me. He would always drive slowly by me so that I could see him. I was only thirteen years old, so what did I really know about relationships? Nothing.

My mom had a talk with me then that changed my life forever. She asked me if I was ready to marry this twenty-one-year-old man who would expect me to drop out of middle school. Yes, I liked his attention, but did I want my life to be like hers? If I decided to be with him, I would most likely have to work in the heat in the fields; wouldn't I rather stay in school? I cried that night, and I told my mom I wanted to study. That was the last time our family migrated to Florida farms.

—◈◈◈—

I am who I am now because my mother gave me the opportunity to study.

—◈◈◈—

I am who I am now because my mother gave me the opportunity to study. She only had a third-grade education in Mexico. My grandmother had pulled her out of school to work so she could help feed the family. I am so grateful my mother gave me the opportunity to earn the education that she did not have. I love my mom so much for all her sacrifices. Those sacrifices do not go unnoticed. I am who I am because my mother wanted something better for me and God was in control.

Chapter 5

SCHOOL AND THE TRAGIC NIGHT

As the years went by, I excelled academically. School was my life, and I thrived in it.

I was invisible during my school years. I was a nobody, not popular, and there was nothing special about me. I was just a good student academically.

I was a basketball player from my freshman year until eleventh grade. In the ninth grade, I was the second tallest female in my class. The team coach wanted me to play, but I was horrible at basketball; I had never even dribbled a ball. Yet, I continued to learn the game.

My senior year, I quit the basketball team to join a mariachi band. My coach told me I was a loser, that only losers quit, but mariachi singing was something I wanted to do. Yes, mariachi are the ones who wear the big sombreros and play guitars. I sang and played an acoustic guitar.

Fast forward to graduation. I sang a song, and my coach heard me sing for the first time. He came up to me afterward and said leaving basketball was the best thing I ever did, that I was a much better singer than I was a basketball player.

Some people will speak things over you or your life that are not true and are hurtful. Some things they say may even be extremely hateful and horrible. Do not receive them. When someone speaks something bad or evil to me, I simply don't receive it. Words have power.

Some people will speak things over you or your life that are not true and are hurtful. Some things they say may even be extremely hateful and horrible. Do not receive them.

Do not let any unwholesome talk come out of your mouths, but only what is helpful for building others up according to their needs, that it may benefit those who listen. (Ephesians 4:29)

A person's words can be life-giving water: words of true wisdom are as refreshing as a bubbling brook. (Proverbs 18:4)

Your own soul is nourished when you are kind, but you destroy yourself when you are cruel. (Proverbs 11:17)

What are you going to do the next time someone speaks something evil or negative to you? I ignore the negative talk of others and reevaluate who my friends are, like you will hopefully. As of this day, I am both strong and confident. We now know words are powerful, so only receive what will uplift you.

I was accepted to Texas A&M in College Station, Texas, and to The University of Texas in Austin. I wanted to get away from my childhood friends, so I chose to go to Texas A&M, where I knew no one. The rest of the graduates went to the party town of Austin. What was I thinking? I would have been partying nonstop in the Live Music Capital of the World if I had gone to Austin. God was taking care of me even when I did not know it.

I made some of my best friends at Texas A&M, but I also trusted some people I shouldn't have. One day, a classmate in my horticulture class said she could drop off my assignment for me. I think I had to go to work and was running late, so I agreed. She ended up cheating off of my paper, and I got put on academic probation.

I was so busy partying and still emotionally starving that I did not focus on my studies. In high school, I had been an honor roll student, but my grades were not good enough for what I needed in college because I kept changing my major and I did not study enough.

As a freshman at Texas A&M, a guy humiliated me in the lunchroom by smacking my butt in front of everyone while he had two women next to him. I was being talked about because I had been talking to a popular guy. I don't know what he was saying about me, but I was still a virgin my freshman year. I walked to my dorm room and told one of the supervisors. They called the cops, and the guy denied everything. The case was dismissed because he knew someone in the university hierarchy who vouched for him. If I knew then what I know

now, I would have taken a different action. Just because I was the poor girl from the country, I was dismissed.

I started partying more to just move on and forget until I was forced to take a semester off. I did not want to stop studying, so I moved to San Antonio, Texas, where I enrolled at the University of Texas at San Antonio (UTSA). I received my bachelor of arts from there on May 10, 1997.

At this point in my life, I was running from God. I dated guys from different religions. I dated Muslim guys and even went into the mosque covered up. I dated an Indian guy who had different beliefs and a different god. I was curious, but something deep down inside me told me I would never marry any of them, and neither would they marry me because of our beliefs. I did not have a relationship with Jesus Christ. I just knew of Him.

Years after my mom's divorce from my father, we went to a local Catholic church. I sang in the choir, and everything was great until the day we were told that because my mom was divorced, I could not be in the choir representing our community. What kind of example would they be setting, we were told. I was angry and bitter toward the Catholic church because this was all that I knew. My mom did not ask to get cheated on. Yes, she made mistakes, but we all do.

For years, I stayed away from all churches. Prior to that, I had done my Holy Communion and Confirmation. I went through the motions of saying the Father, the Son, and the Holy Spirit while I made the sign of the cross. That is all I learned in the Catholic Church; I didn't even remember what they represented because I had these sacraments at a young age.

What I knew of the Holy Spirit was limited. Up until age 30, all Catholicism had taught me was how to make the cross on my forehead. I did not know of the power of God, the gifts of the spirit, or anything about God's healing and forgiveness. When I walked out of the Sunday mass, it was back to my sinful, pathetic life of party, party, party. An emptiness consumed me.

I have nothing against the Catholic Church; I have even

I stooped pretty low because I had low self-esteem.

visited the Vatican, and it is beautiful. I was just meant to go through this to be where I am at now. I believe you can go to any church as long as you are connected with God.

The Catholic Church was not solving my issues or leading me to a better spiritual life. Later on, someone from that same church who pushed us away called and said we could come back. I did not, but it is good that they called.

During the years that this happened, I was consumed by anger and misery. I am sure I was rude and hurt people. I sinned, I drank, and I was promiscuous. I stooped pretty low because I had low self-esteem. I am guilty of many things, and today I speak directly to you. If I hurt you in any way, then I ask you to forgive me. I am not the same person I was back then. I am not perfect, but I have made peace with my past. Please forgive me.

Chapter 6

MY FIRST PRAYER

While I was in San Antonio at UTSA, I was more focused on my academics. I had to pay for my apartment and food, so I worked at a restaurant with a bar. One night, I went out on a date, and I wore a short yellow dress with flowers and spaghetti straps. My date was a Hispanic guy from my small hometown, so I felt I could trust him in this big city.

He picked me up at my place and drove us to his home, which was a trailer. That night he raped me. I told him to stop, and I cried at his place. He said I was asking for it because I had worn that dress. I felt ashamed and told only a few of my coworkers and my friend.

Shame kept me bound for years. I did not report the rape to the police because I was ashamed. I did not want people to know what had happened to me. I will never forget that night. I was hurt and angry at God for letting it happen to me. I remember looking up to heaven and saying, "God, I know that I am not perfect, but I was not bad either. How could you let this happen to me? From this moment on, I don't want to know anything of You. I hate You."

That was the first time in my life I got drunk. I remember getting a chicken sandwich at a drive-thru. That was the beginning of my toxic years.

Pushing God away was the worst thing I could have ever done. For the next phase of my life, which was about seven or eight years, God was silent. I was vulnerable in a world that did not love me. I started drinking heavily from that day on. I used alcohol to forget and not feel the pain I was in.

I went from relationship to relationship, never finding the love I desired. I had men who wanted me for all the wrong reasons. Years passed until one day, I was at my point of surrender. It had been the same cycle of being involved with men who did not appreciate me and who were abusive or cheaters.

During those years without God, I was in a toxic relationship where I was beaten by my ex-boyfriend. He had told me that he needed to get married by a certain date to be able to get a visa to stay in the United States legally. I had stopped loving him and no longer wanted to have sex with him, so he started hitting me in the face. All I wanted to do was find something to defend myself with, but there was nothing within my reach. I was shocked that he was hitting me with his fist because he had loved me; how could he be hurting me now? He did not stop hurting me until my sister heard my screams and busted my door open. Gladys came in yelling at him. He had been drinking that night, and when my sister came in yelling, he reacted as if he knew he had crossed the line and ran to the front door. He could have been deported or lost his opportunity to stay in America.

I called the cops, but I did not press charges with the San Antonio Police Department because I was scared that my ex-boyfriend would hurt me or my sister. My sister and I had no other family or friends to protect us. It was just us in a big city. This was a horrible and shameful time in my life.

Time passed, and one Saturday night, I did the unthinkable. The night before, I had ended my relationship with a military guy I had been dating. He was a Christian guy, and I wanted a serious relationship. He told me he could not give me what I wanted because of his career, so I walked away.

That Saturday night, I remember I wore my warm ups. I had not shaved; my legs were prickly. I had just broken up, so you can imagine how horrible I felt. I had the puffy eye look because I had cried during the night.

I was in my cozy little apartment when my sister Gladys called me. She told me to get ready because she wanted us to go out so I would forget about the night before. I told her I was not going because I realized that time after time of doing the same thing, nothing would change. I realized I no longer wanted to do it on my own.

Remember when I said I did the unthinkable? I, the woman who had run from God for thirty years, finally got on my knees and said, "Lord, if You exist, send me a man who loves You more than he loves me, and I will follow You. I will give up the drinking and partying."

My tears burned as they ran down my cheeks. I approached my computer and pulled up my online dating profile. I was ready to hit the delete button when a message popped up. The person had typed to me, "I love God above all things." He told me verbatim what I had just prayed for. I took it as a sign.

Nothing is impossible for God. I may have been wrong for asking Him to prove himself like that, but He was graceful and merciful with me, and He made it happen. I encourage you that no matter what your situation is, you too can ask Him. Speak to Him and let Him know how you feel. You have nothing to lose, but get ready when He answers you.

Chapter 7

MY MARRIAGE

My new life began in 2003. I relocated to Orlando, Florida, to get to know the man I had met online that night of my prayer. Goodbye, Spurs; hello, Orlando Magic! In only a few months, I married the man who had sent me that message. It all sounds so perfect, right? Well, I sure thought it was going to be. After all, he was a Christian man, so why wouldn't it? He loved God, he spoke in tongues, he listened to gospel music, and he had never drunk a sip of alcohol in his entire life. I thought I was the luckiest woman alive.

We married, but our marriage was not a happy one. I did not realize that the woman he had been with prior to me would interfere in our marriage for over a year. His previous lover had been in an abusive relationship, so I can only imagine that it was her who kept the contact going, but even if it was not, I no longer care. My husband told me they were still in contact, but I am not sure if it was by phone or email. I also don't know if he was sleeping with her. He purposefully did not set boundaries with her, and

the constant disrespect to me was an issue. That made me not trust him, and I felt insecure.

During our marriage, my husband questioned if I had the Holy Spirit. The truth is I did not know the answer myself. My husband made me feel that I was unworthy. I wish I could tell you that things turned around, but the reality is my brokenness and unforgiveness toward my father were hindering my marriage.

How could I love when I had such bitterness and other dreadful feelings all over me? I prayed about it, and then one day, I told God I could no longer do it. The hate toward my father was still negatively impacting me. I told God that it was on Him and I could not do it anymore. I surrendered my pain to Him. I got on my knees and wept like a baby.

At my husband's advice, I looked for my dad to get closure and healing. My siblings had been in contact with him, so I got my sister to send a message to my father. I was ready to talk and ask why he left me. I needed to know why I was not good enough for him to come back to. What had I done that was so wrong that he did not love me enough to come back? These were some of the questions on my mind. I called my dad and left him a message.

My dad called me while I was at work at a cell phone company. I remember stepping to the back room and taking a seat for the phone call. We both cried. I told him I was Sandra, his thirty-year-old daughter. I was the prideful one, the one who hated him, the one who called him a sperm donor all her life. I told him I was angry at him for never being around. How dare he just walk away from our lives and move on to raise another family? He had remarried and had another two daughters and a son.

He listened to me, and then he said, "I am so sorry, Mija," which means "daughter." I sobbed like a baby. He apologized to me and asked if I could forgive him. I told him I was not God and that only God could forgive him. Up until that call, I had a dark heart. Hate had consumed me, all of me. The day I talked with my father, I felt something being released from me. The hate and bitterness left me all at once. I felt a peace I had never felt before.

The day I talked with my father, I felt something being released from me. The hate and bitterness left me all at once. I felt a peace I had never felt before.

Do not be anxious about anything, but in everything by prayer and supplication with thanksgiving let your requests be made known to God...Therefore confess your sins to one another and pray for one another, that you may be healed. The prayer of the righteous person has great power as it is working. (Philippians 4:6-7)

Then they cried to the Lord in their trouble, and he delivered them from their distress. He made the storm be still, and the waves of the sea were hushed. Then they were glad that the waters were quiet, and he brought them to their desired haven. (Psalm 107:28-30)

And whatever you ask in prayer, you will receive, if you have faith. (Matthew 21:22)

Therefore I tell you, whatever you ask in prayer, believe that you have received it, and it will be yours. (Mark 11:24)

At this point in my life, I did not believe in divorce for any reason, so my marriage continued. I told myself that no matter what problems arose, I would stay with my husband because I did not want my baby to be without her father the way I had been.

I shared earlier what happened during my pregnancy with my baby girl. After going through all that and having delivered my precious daughter, I was moved into the hospital room where I would recover and eat the hospital food. When I had my daughter in my arms, my husband stood in the back of the room and said, "Sandra, I have something to tell you." I listened, and he proceeded to tell me that he had been talking another woman, but because of our newborn, he would stop talking to her.

I was stunned and upset. How could this man be so cruel and hurt me like this? This was supposed to be the best day of my life, and he destroyed that. I collected my strength and composure, then asked him if he loved her. For a few minutes that seemed everlasting, he stayed quiet, then said he would end it. My heart went numb; he did not even respond to the question I had asked.

At home, things were not the same. He worked the nightshift, and I worked the dayshift, so we slept in separate rooms. We might as well have been roommates because there was no love. We would have sex and not even kiss. It was just disgusting and hurtful to know I was married and unloved; however, because of my past and not having my dad present in my childhood, I was willing to put up with anything.

Our second child came in December 2006. Before he was born, I was told I needed to have an abortion. At an early stage of my pregnancy, the doctor detected a thickened nuchal fold. My unborn child had a high percentage of having Down syndrome. I told the doctor I was going to have my baby no matter what.

From the time I got married and for about the next seven years, my husband kept saying I needed to change. I did not know what he was talking about; I had this face of confusion when he said that. I worked, took care of the two kids, and went to church, the gym, and home. I had no friends outside of work, and I was just a boring, predictable wife. In my mind, I was a strong woman. Perhaps I could have been a better cook or kept the house neater. Would that have made a difference?

All I knew was my husband was never happy with me. When I got home, he was ready to fight over any little thing I did. He always had an issue with my weight. Back then, I was eighty to one hundred pounds lighter than what I am now, and he still complained. He made me think I was never good enough for him.

The fighting continued, and I started to think God had played a joke on me by allowing me to marry a man who did not love me. My husband told me he wanted a pure wife; I was not a virgin, and I had been sexually active with other men before marriage. He had never had a drink in his life, and in my opinion, I was the opposite of what he had asked God for; I had been the partier. My ex would tell me I was not "the one," that I was "damaged goods."

Surely God made a mistake, I thought. One year passed, and I had become distant and unloving toward him. No marriage is one sided. I made plenty of mistakes and poor decisions. I withheld sex from my husband if I was upset, to simply prove my point, or to just not give in. That was wrong of me. These are some of the excuses I used to deny my husband sex:

1. I have my period (even when I was not).
2. Honey, I have a headache.
3. My back hurts.
4. The kids need to do their homework or take a shower.
5. I need to do the laundry (or any type of housework).

I now know what the Bible says about this behavior.

Do not deprive each other of sexual relations, unless you both agree to refrain…Do not deny yourselves to each other, unless you first agree to do so for a while. (1 Corinthians 7:5)

I know I was wrong. I used sex as a weapon. When sex is being withheld or we get too busy to not make our husband feel special or satisfied, I guarantee you there is a woman elsewhere ready to tell your man something sweet or lure him with sex since he is craving it.

During the time of our separation prior to divorcing, my ex told me something that was hard to hear but very useful for me. He said the reason he loved his ex-girlfriend over me was because she made him feel like a king. He said I did not need him and I just wanted him, and to him, that was a turn off.

As much as I hated to hear it, I am glad he shared it with me. This taught me a valuable lesson. I learned that

I could be strong and independent, but a wife is supposed to make her husband feel that she needs him for sex, love, and companionship. I was supposed to make him feel that without him, my life would not be as great as it is with him. I know some of you are probably making faces just like I was, but hear me out. I get it. Trust me.

I grew up thinking I could do it on my own. I was determined to make it regardless of my tough life. I had a survivor mentality, but I learned that a part of being married means honoring my promise to love my husband and do what I need to do to make him happy.

What could I have done differently? I could have asked him for more help and assistance with what I was doing. I should have supported his dreams or stopped what I was doing to listen to what he wanted to share. I could have asked for his opinion on things relating to the family. I could have remarked on how strong he was and made him feel good because he was a good provider. I could have, and could have again, but I did not. I was wrong so many times, and I accept this now. I accept that I too am responsible for the demise of my marriage.

What my husband did not know is that I was starving for affection, to be loved and touched. I knew if I tried to do something freaky in bed with him, it would start a problem because he always judged me for my past and threw it right back in my face. So yes, I was the boring, predictable wife.

Years passed, and my husband and I remained distant. I had grown tired of him saying things like, "Just wait and see," with a smirk. It was his way of making me feel that he could not trust me and that he was up to something. However, God was and is always in control of my life.

Chapter 8

MY EMOTIONAL
INFIDELITY

I worked at a bank as a manager. I loved helping clients and motivating my team. There was one particular client who would come in to our branch often. I was getting no attention at home, and here was this handsome, married man coming into my workplace always looking for me. He was educated, muscular, and just charming. He smelled so good too. He wanted my attention, which made me feel special. I would ask my team members to assist him so I could avoid him. I found myself liking the attention he was giving me, so I was trying to avoid temptation. He was persistent. Most of the time, he would wait until I was finished helping other clients so that I could help him with his banking needs.

This man and I never physically did more than just shake hands, yet I was emotionally attracted to him. When I thought about him, it made me happy. Was I right to be feeling like this? Absolutely not! Emotional infidelity is wrong, and it hurt my marriage.

One time at the YMCA, my husband and I were working out. That man was there, and my husband noticed that he was staring at us. He made it a point to get close to me. My husband, who rarely touched me, was holding me by my waist. The other guy left, all upset and jealous. I told my husband the gym guy was the same one who had been giving me attention at work. It was clear my husband did not love me because he told me to go and get attention from that guy, that he did not care.

Since I found myself thinking of this guy, I knew that things had to stop or I would fall into more sin. I addressed it with the man, and we stopped talking altogether. He made it sound like it was all in my imagination. I never should have ever allowed myself to get distracted by that man.

Let me be very clear: this was cheating, no matter what way I put it. This was wrong. Be careful about doing something like this because it is emotional infidelity.

Men and women are not naive. A person knows when your mind is on someone else. For example, maybe you get dressed more seductively for work than for your own spouse. I knew the guy was a married man, yet he was pure temptation for me. I reminded him I was a married woman and I had no plans of ever crossing any lines with him. He, in turn, made it seem like there was nothing going on. I am glad that things shifted and we both went on with our own lives. He stopped waiting for me at the bank, and we went on as if nothing had ever happened. When we saw each other at the YMCA or anywhere else, we just ignored each other.

Again, emotional infidelity is wrong. Sin is sin, and we know it, so no more sugar coating it. I was wrong, and I repent.

The same applies to online dating sites. Even if you are not physically seeing the person yet but you are texting, sending pictures, sending kisses, or giving yourself emotionally to anyone other than your spouse, it is cheating.

If you are married and busy exchanging pictures with someone else, even if you've never met that person, then it is cheating. Think of all the apps online and on your phone and what you are doing with them. Let's cut the bull. If your spouse was doing the same thing with someone else, how would that make you feel? Or better yet, would you trust your spouse with your cell phone unlocked all day or for a week? Be real. If the answer is no, then check yourself.

If your best friend is texting risqué messages and pictures, then you need to be a good friend and tell them to stop if they are married. There is a line called respect we should not cross. If your husband or wife is busy liking all these women or men on any online app, then you need to address it. I know that it hurts or maybe you feel lonely—I get it because I have been there—but it is important because I learned my lesson.

God is always going to give you a way out. Remember that.

God is always going to give you a way out. Remember that.

And God is faithful; he will not let you be tempted beyond what you can bear. But when you are tempted, he will also provide a way out so that you can endure it. (1 Corinthians 10:13)

One day, I came home early from work. My husband had gone to pick up our son from daycare, and he had left his browser open on his computer. There was a collage of women he had been talking to. Could I blame him? I blame myself more. Anger came over me. I was a heated Latina ready to hurt him. When he returned with our son, I told him what I had seen and walked him to the door. I told him to get out. This started our separation.

I waited that first year, still thinking that things would change—after all, he had said he was working on himself. My life continued with my kids. They became my only focus. My priorities shifted from my work to making my family my first priority. My husband blamed me in the past because I focused so much on work. I did so because that was the only thing I thought I was good at; my husband complained about everything else.

I had been with my employer for more than 10 years. I stepped down from bank manager to assistant manager because I was an emotional mess. Six months later, my position was eliminated. I humbly accepted my role as a personal banker. I wanted a healthy balance with work and home. My kids were three and five years old. My marriage was already broken, and my husband resented me for choosing my career over my family. Keeping him happy was out of my control because he was never happy with me. What happened to him saying, "Sure, I will support you in your career?"

We remained separated for two years and three months until we were finally divorced. The day I went to the courthouse to ask if the papers had been signed and recorded, the clerk told me, "Sandra, the divorce has been filed, and you are a single woman." I was so happy.

I believe in the covenant of marriage with all my heart. My divorce did not break me; it just taught me a lesson or two. I am grateful for everything that happened regardless of the pain I had to endure. I have two beautiful children. My ex-husband has remarried, and I love his wife. He met an amazing woman of God who loves our children like her own.

My ex is a good father, and that is all that matters. People need to stop using their kids to hurt the other person when the relationship between them doesn't work out. I am who I am now because of some of the life lessons I learned while with my ex. To my ex, thank you for everything, and I am sorry I hurt you. Thanks for helping me become who I now am.

I need to trust that God has a purpose for everything. If I had known this was going to be the outcome of my marriage, I would have done some things differently much sooner. I trust God with all my heart, and I thank Him for my yesterday, today, and tomorrow.

Chapter 9

HURT BY THE CHURCH

As my marriage was falling apart, I continued to attend a charismatic church. It was not just a church; it became my family. We were small in number yet strong in the Spirit, and we thirsted for God. Everyone knew everything about each other (well, almost everything). We all sought God wholeheartedly.

The pastor was unlike anyone I had met before. She was a beautiful person inside and out; however, I was always an outsider and not in her inner circle. That made me feel a little hurt, but I accepted it, and God's love kept me going.

This woman of God prayed for me, and my situation turned around. I thought I was going to lose my house, but God turned things around and I was able to keep it. You see, my house had black mold in the downstairs master bedroom closet. I did not know about it because I did not use this room. I slept in a different room upstairs to be close to my kids. When I made my first insurance claim in over a decade, my home insurance denied it. Here I was in a home that was not safe for my kids, full of old memories and so much negative equity.

I also was engulfed in debt because I often went out and bought something in order to make myself feel good. This was a bad behavior from my childhood—trying to fill a void with something else is not right.

I had always paid my bills and was responsible with money. Before becoming overwhelmed with debt, my credit score had been in the 800s. I prided myself on that. My husband had taught me about credit. I preached having a good credit score at work, and then all of this happened.

The mortgage crisis hit us all, but my county was devastated by this crisis. My home lost half of its equity, and I owed more on it than it was worth. I reached out to the credit union to work with me on my home equity and reduce my payments, but they refused. I asked if I could do a short sale where the outstanding debt would be forgiven, and the bank said no. With my back against the wall, and after looking at all my options, I decided to file for bankruptcy. The local credit union said that even if I sold my home, I would still have to pay a substantial amount, and they would not want to forgive the debt. Declaring bankruptcy was my only way to keep my home and get a fresh start. I declared bankruptcy and lost my credit. This was emotionally difficult.

I hired an attorney, and in three months, my mortgage payment was adjusted to an affordable payment. I thank God for this. I went from having my kids in a private school when I was married to having to send them to a free charter school because I could no longer afford the tuition on my single salary. This was a humbling transition for me because I could afford to buy almost anything we wanted when I was married. Now, I had to think twice about what I spent my money on.

My best friend and I had been attending a small, local church for years. I felt I was being talked about at church because I was not the holy type in the way I dressed or behaved, meaning I may have worn a dress where my shoulders were visible.

I was just beginning my single life, and I had started to date. I should have listened to the pastor because she had told me to be patient and faithful to God. She suggested that I not sin, but the lust of the flesh got the better of me. I had one foot in the church and one in the world. I looked forward to going out and having fun.

I began to keep to myself and pushed forward with work and family. It is one thing to be corrected in private and another thing to always be made a show of it. I felt I was constantly picked on.

One day, the pastor called me to confront me as to why I was talking about her. I told her I didn't know what she was talking about and neither did I have time to be talking about people. I told her my life was busy with other things happening and that I did not have time to be gossiping about anyone, especially her. Not to sound rude, but I just did not care about the nonsense happening in the church when I knew that was not what church should be about. The pastor and I agreed that it was best to cut all ties.

I left the church and decided to not return to that ministry. Little did I know I would lose my best friend of ten years in the process of my leaving. It was one thing to lose the church but another thing to lose her friendship. I had no family in the city I lived in, and my best friend was like a sister. It hurt so much to lose her.

When I look back at my time at the church and with the pastor, I was wrong for many things. I know God used her in so many ways, and she was kind to many people. I think I just had to go through what I did so that my personal relationship with God could begin. I will forever be grateful to that pastor for all her time and love. Correction is good, but at the time, I was not ready to hear it.

Chapter 10

GOD IS A JEALOUS GOD

For three years, I stayed away from the church. One lesson I learned is that God is a jealous God. When you put others before God, He gets jealous. I was wrong to have lived one step inside the church and one step out. That is not right, and I was called out for it. The pastor did what was right, but in my stubbornness, I did not take things well.

In prior years, I had put my best friend first. When I had a problem, I sought her. When something good happened, I ran to tell her. In those three years after leaving,

━━━◦◦◦━━━

One lesson I learned is that God is a jealous God. When you put others before God, He gets jealous.

━━━◦◦◦━━━

when I had no one, God became my everything. God was my Father and my number one. I talked to Him as if He could hear me. If I had a good day at work, I told Him. If I had a bad day, I told Him that too.

This all happened for a reason. Before my separation from the church, I did not seek God other than while in church. I thank that pastor because I was meant to go through this period with God to be where I am in my relationship with Him today. God wants us to trust Him. He is with me daily, not just when I attend church.

The beauty of friendship is that you can pick up where things have left off and continue moving forward. There is always forgiveness and restitution with the Lord, so even though we may not understand everything at the moment it occurs, there is a reason for it. Ask yourself, what is the purpose or reason you were meant to go through what you are going though? What did you learn from it?

I struggled with the pain of not being fully accepted and loved for many years. If you are in a church that likes to gossip or judge others, please stop gossiping, and don't add fuel to the fire. There are many people who want God regardless of how they appear, speak, or behave. We are not the wardrobe patrol. It is we who have pushed away many people who are seeking God. It is time to change. There is no perfect church, and we need to stop the bickering and judgment. Let's pray for each other instead and love each other more, uplifting each other and going forward with positive vibes.

It's now October 2020, and I have found a local church that put on their website that people can wear anything from business casual to shorts and sandals. I am encouraged to know this because it gives me hope that the past will not repeat itself over something so meaningless.

There is always forgiveness and restitution with the Lord, so even though we may not understand everything at the moment it occurs, there is a reason for it.

One other thing that has been in my spirit I understand that this year of COVID-19 has been a terrible year for many of us. Some may have lost friends and family members and others their jobs. I lost my stepmother this year. I understand how tough things may be. Don't lose faith.

For others, stop making your job your God. Make time for God. Stay in prayer and God will provide all your needs. Here are some verses proving that God will provide:

And my God will supply every need of yours according to his riches in glory in Christ Jesus. (Philippians 4:19)

And without faith it is impossible to please him, for whoever draw near to God must believe that he exists and that he rewards those who seek him. (Hebrews 11:6)

The Lord does not let the righteous go hungry, but he thwarts the craving of the wicked. (Proverbs 10:3)

But seek first the kingdom of God and his righteousness, and all these things will be added to you. (Matthew 6:33)

For I know the plans I have for you, declares the Lord, plans for welfare and not for evil, to give you a future and a hope. (Jeremiah 29:11)

The young lions suffer want and hunger; but those who seek the LORD lack no good thing. (Psalm 34:10)

Therefore I tell you, do not be anxious about your life, what you will eat or what you will drink, nor about your body, what you will put on. Is not life more than food, and the body more than clothing? Look at the birds of the air: they neither sow nor reap nor gather into barns, and yet your heavenly Father feeds them. Are you not of more value than they? And which of you by being anxious about clothing? Consider the lilies of the field, how they grow: they neither toil nor spin, yet I tell you, even Solomon in all his glory was not arrayed like one of these... (Matthew 6:25-34)

Chapter 11

ASKING GOD FOR A SIGN

When I was not attending church, I met a Jamaican man. He was so handsome and tall. We immediately connected and entered into a lustful relationship. I stayed with this guy for four or five months. In that timeframe, he asked me to marry him three times. He said it was so easy to love me. Finally, I was hearing the words that melted my heart and I yearned to hear.

He worked but had no car, so at times I would get up extra early to drop him off at his job. Then one day, we went to the mall and he picked out some clothes. He then looked at me and asked me to pay for them. I did not, but it caused me to think twice about what his intentions were with me.

I know I am a giving person; however, I am not naive. I loved him, but I knew he was trying to use me because of how he said I needed to buy those clothes while we were at the register. I was so desperate for love that I was willing to ignore some signs when I knew better than that. We know when someone is good for us and when someone is just using us.

I had strayed away from God, and I was sinning. In my quest for love and companionship, I settled for a man who was taking me back to what I had come out of, specifically the drinking and the partying. Twice I heard the Holy Spirit tell me to leave him, and I said, "But Lord, I love him." Around the time that I was in this toxic relationship, there were two nights that I was in deep sleep and I woke up in panic because I heard the sound of chains being wrapped around my feet. I was terrified, but I remembered that the name of Jesus has Power. I screamed, "Jesus," and the sound of rattling chains stopped. Another night, I felt the same thing and heard the same noises, except that this time, I felt that my chest was being pressed down. Again, I screamed, "Jesus." Then there was calmness. I could say that I was dreaming, but I know that would be me denying what happened. Something was trying to bind me, and I thank God that the plan of the enemy did not work.

Then one day, two local pastors and a pastor from Nigeria came to my workplace. They invited me to come to church that Wednesday. Something happened to me, and I was restless that day. I needed a word from God. I wanted a word from God. I went to their church on Wednesday unannounced. I sat in the back and just listened.

Then it all began. Pastor Mike Akwundi from Nigeria began to prophesy to me. He was on point with what he shared with me, and I knew God was using him to speak to me. Pastor Akwundi said God was asking me why I had not finished the assignment He had given me. I knew he was referring to this book. Pastor Akwundi also said others had intentionally hurt me. I left the service that night on fire, spiritually speaking.

My desire to serve God was strong enough to forget my past pains, and I said this mighty prayer: "Lord, if there is anything in my life that is preventing me from moving forward with You and my destiny, cut it from the root, Lord. You now have my heart, and I want You, Lord, all of You." That was on that Wednesday. By Saturday, I had broken up with my boyfriend.

One time he called me, and I heard a girl in the background. He, of course, denied that. I went to work, and for four days, I cried because I was hurting. So, I got up after the fourth day, and I talked to God. I told Him, "Lord, You told me to let him go, and I did, but I am still hurting. I need to know why, or I will go back. So, if You love me, Lord, show me why I needed to break up with him." Be careful what you ask of God because sometimes you may not want to see the signs He gives you.

My ex-boyfriend was still sending me daily text messages of "I love you," so it was hard to forget him. Plus, I was being stubborn and not letting him go out of my heart. The day I said the prayer above, I went to work determined to see him that afternoon and talk.

When I went to see him, there was another woman there. She asked me who I was, and I responded that I was his girlfriend. She asked me for how long, and I told her it had been four or five months. She asked how I could be his girlfriend when she was also his girlfriend. Yes, you heard me. "His girlfriend," she said. I told her she could have him because I no longer wanted him, that only a dog eats its own vomit. I was upset. There is no need to share the rest of this episode other than it was a hard lesson to experience. Next time, I will listen to God.

I learned God was saving me from a cheating man. Sometimes, we choose to be with people we know will take us away from the things of God. God gives us a choice. You have one life and a decision to make.

My attorney once asked me why I had chosen my boyfriend over being with someone else who could have given the healthy relationship I needed. He told me of the broken wing syndrome. Up until then, I did not know that I had been choosing men that needed fixing or nurturing.

I had heard of many men looking for women that were abused, broken, and in emotional need because they wanted to be the ones to fix them. I just had not thought that I could do the same. *Not me,* I thought, but I was wrong. Trying to rescue someone or fix them is not gender specific.

Author Savannah Grey wrote in Esteemology the article "Why You Should Avoid the Fixer-Upper Man and the Broken Wing Theory" (https://esteemology.com/why-you-should-avoid-the-fixer-upper-man-and-the-broken-wing-theory/), which states that the broken wing theory is when he dangles everything you want right in front of you. He puts all of his energy and attention on you. He's the perfect guy. He pursues you like no one ever has, and because you are a nurturer, all you want to do is throw your arms around him and say, "Aww, you poor, misunderstood baby. Let me take care of you. Let me make it all better."

My ex-boyfriend and I had a toxic relationship that was leading me the wrong way. I am glad God intervened and saved me from that mess. After all that, I shed no more tears, none for him. I moved on very fast, trust me. What did I learn from this? I needed to stop trying to fix people when I should focus on myself first. Pray and seek God when it comes to you and your relationships. God hears you.

To all the people in my past who hurt me, judged me, talked about me, and took advantage of me, I forgive you.

To anyone I have offended or hurt, I ask for your forgiveness. I was wrong, and I accept my responsibility.

As of right now, I walk away with a pure heart. I surrendered it all to God a long time ago. It's time to move forward.

Chapter 12
MY DAD'S LETTER

As of the time of this writing, my dad has now been in my life for fifteen years. My dad and I are not best friends or anything, but he is my dad, and I love him. I am attaching a letter from my dad where he shares his story.

My military dad.

Name: Gustavo

I grew up working in the fields as a migrant farm worker. My family and I would go to west Texas, Arkansas, Delaware, Maryland, and Illinois. I often missed the first three or four months of school, but I would catch up and surpass my fellow classmates in order to succeed and achieve.

I first married on December 1, 1969, at seventeen years old. My first baby girl was born in October 1971.

I was drafted into the army in November 1972 and was sent to basic training in Louisiana. I was then transferred to advanced infantry training at El Paso, Texas. From there I was sent to Korea. I was still in Korea in May 1973 when my second baby girl was born.

On February 1974, I was sent home. That same month, my first wife and I separated, never to get together again. When going through the divorce, I had no idea I was going to be a father for the third time. I found out later I had a son born on February 9, 1975.

I went to technical school where I graduated and got a job in accounting for a CPA. I worked there for two-and-a-half years.

On or about March 1977, I started reading the New Testament, and the Lord found it in His heart to save me. I accepted Jesus Christ as my Lord and Savior.

On July 2, 1977, I remarried for the second time in my life to a Christian young lady. I continued serving the Lord with all my heart and soul. I learned to love the Lord and depended on Him to help and guide me in His ways.

My job as an accountant ended, and I started looking for another one. I applied for a position as a loan officer, and I was hired. On June 15, 1980, the first daughter from my second marriage was born. On November 30,1981, another daughter was born. I had a son on February 9, 1985, the same day as my first was born but 10 years apart.

In December 1994, my second wife and I got into a big disagreement/argument, which resulted in our separation. We did not get together again, and we divorced in February 2006. I married my third and final wife in July 2006.

In January 1992, I started working for the Donna Independent School District. I continued working there for 1 month short of 26 years. I retired on December 21, 2017.

I was the first person in my family to accept the Lord Jesus Christ. One of my main prayers was for all of my brothers, sisters, Mom, and Dad to accept the Lord as their Savior. As time went by, my family could see that God was answering my prayers. My brothers, sisters, and mother accepted the Lord as their Savior.

As both my families started to get older, I talked to my second family, asking them to try to contact their brother and sisters. It was hard going. Neither family really wanted to do that. At the age of six-ty-five, it finally happened. Sandra kept telling her sisters that she wanted to meet with them.

At that time, my oldest daughter was forty-five years of age. I asked one of my daughters to do me the biggest favor I would ever ask of her. It was to meet each other as brothers and sisters. She complied with my request. Each and every one of them agreed.

By that time, my oldest daughter had not spoken to me in twenty years. She had two sons and they were asking to meet her father, but at that time, she told them she didn't have a father anymore. What she had told her boys kept bugging her mind and heart. She asked her sister to ask me to call her, and I did. I called her right away, and we started to call and text each other.

A little while later, I asked Sandra to ask her brother to meet with their other brother and sisters from my second family. After a lot of prayer, on June 17, 2017, both my families met for the very first time. It was the greatest day of my life, as if my children were reborn again into my life. We continue to talk and enjoy each other.

God is great! God is so good.

Chapter 13

WHY THE LIES OF CHILD SUPPORT?

The reason I want to talk about child support is because this is a topic that sometimes parents do not handle properly. In my parents' divorce, there was an established amount set in place. It was a very small amount, and regardless of what the amount was, my mother always used to tell us that my dad did not love us, which is why he did not pay child support.

Now imagine how much those words made me hate my father even more than what I already did. That there was no child support is all I would remember for the next twenty-three years from the time I was seven years old.

When I was growing up, part of me wondered if my father ever thought of me or if he, at any point, regretted leaving my older sister, myself, and my younger brother. I knew he was a provider for his second family, and here my mom was telling us that he did not even pay child support. That made me so angry because we were living off government assistance and did not have enough money for food and clothes at times. A happy memory is getting the block of cheese from the WIC program. I don't know why I remember that, but I do.

During the family reunion in Texas in June 2017, my stepsisters told me that my dad had always supplied child support. It was $100 a month he paid for all three of us. They said it was their mom who told him to continue paying the $100. I thanked them for it, but I also felt a little regret because I had been jealous of them since all I knew is that he had raised them and not us. They shared some details as to their childhood. I connected with my stepsisters, and one of them even did my makeup that day. I am so grateful for the opportunity. My stepsiblings are all kindhearted. I am glad I got to meet them at my forty-three years of age.

Back to talking about child support. Do I blame my dad for paying such a small amount of child support? I think there are rules in place that both parents need to follow involving child support. It was my mom's pride and ignorance that led to us not being given the correct amount of financial support from our father. I do remember an attorney coming to our family home once and telling my mom that, based on my dad's income, he owed at least $38,000 in child support. My mom responded, "If I didn't need him when my kids were young, what makes you think that I need him now?" (At this time, we were much older.)

Growing up, we bought our clothes from consignment shops. Sometimes, we had no food. We had a poor life, and if my mother had gotten the proper child support set up, who knows how that would have impacted us. I did ask my mom why she lied to us all those years about her not getting any child support. It was probably not my place to even ask her that question, but being told my father did not provide financially and was a deadbeat dad made me resent him more. Parents should not lie about this to their kids because when a child hates, it is something they carry for life unless a miracle happens.

Today, I am so grateful to God for everything He has done for me. Good and bad, it has made me into the woman I am today. I love who I am now. I love my kids so much, and I work to give them what I can. To all the people who think life is always bad, seek God and trust Him. My relationship with God is a special one now. I am going to share my miracles so you can see and believe that if He did it for me, He can do it for you. It is just one prayer away.

Chapter 14

MY CREDIT

In 2014, I was struggling financially. I went from being a bank manager to a personal banker. Becoming a single parent made me step down and choose to have a forty-hour job so that I could be there for my kids. I had a decent income; however, my credit was still low because I had filed for bankruptcy.

After the bankruptcy, I could not get approved for any credit cards because I had not restored my credit. I was on a cash-only basis for years. Part of me was scared to get back into credit card debt knowing I only had my income to cover the bills. I did get child support, which helped provide essentials for my kids. I knew that I needed good credit because I eventually want to be approved for an auto loan for the luxury SUV I wanted because my kids were tall, and I wanted to refinance my home.

But in 2014, my credit was bad. I had gotten behind on my mortgage payments because I had spent the money on home and auto repairs. When you are a homeowner, things arise that need fixing. A lot of things in my home broke in 2013. My house definitely needed many home repairs.

In the process of my divorce, the judge said she did not want my mortgage to be reaffirmed. What that means is that my mortgage payment at that time was very high. The judge wanted to help me out by allowing me to have the time that was necessary for my attorney to be able to work out a lower payment that would enable me to keep my home. The downfall to not reaffirming my mortgage is that from that moment on, my payments would not be reported to the credit bureaus. So, for years, I made my payments and it looked like I did not even own my home on my credit report.

One night, I could not sleep knowing I needed money for food. I had blessed someone with my son's bed because there was a family who needed it more, and I had not been able to replace Joshua's bed yet. It also was stressing me that it was time to rebuild my credit and I had not been able to. I had been denied on credit card applications.

There was a guy I had dated a while back, and we had stayed in contact. He was very successful and made more than $100,000 a year as a registered nurse. Upon hearing of how I was struggling financially, he told me he liked me and that I was only struggling because I wanted to. He said he would gladly pay my mortgage so long as I gave him sex. Let me be real—I thought about it for a moment. What would a parent not do if it meant feeding their kids? I would do anything, but I know the God I serve, so I told him I was not interested and that I would trust God.

I got on my knees, and I started to pray. I said, "Lord, You said You are my God and You are a God of miracles. You said, Lord, I can ask You for anything and, if it is in

Your will, that it would be done. Well, Father, I need You now. You know my struggles and my needs. I need You to show up, God, and help me with my finances by helping me put food on the table and allowing my boy to have his bed. In Jesus's name, I pray."

I then stood up and went to my laptop to fill out a credit application for a furniture company. My credit score then was around a 580. Dropping from the 800s to the 500s was so humbling. My fingers slowly typed in the required information, and then I got to the submit button. I stopped, took a deep breath, and said, "It's on You." The online application started to process and APPROVED popped up on the screen. "Congratulations, you have been approved, and your credit score is 785."

There was no way my credit score was 785, but I was so happy my application was accepted. "Oh my gosh, He did it," I said, but then I feared it was just a coincidence. How many of us ask God for a sign or miracle and, when He gives it to us, we question it? I did it at that very moment. Shame on me.

I then said, "Lord, I know You heard me. If You did it once, You can do it again." I then went to a credit card site and again typed in my information. When I got to the submit button, my eyes were wide open. The word "processing" came up on my screen, then "approved for $500.00." I dropped to the floor and started to cry. I said, "Lord, forgive me. I should have trusted You the first time and not doubted You."

I do not know if you or someone you know has ever struggled with their finances. God gave me a credit miracle. I know credit; I am a banker and have been a bank manager.

If you have any questions about what reports to your credit report, go to www.annualcreditreport.com. Click on all three credit bureaus and find out what is being reported on your credit. It is free unless you want your credit score.

What did I learn from my financial hardship? I learned it is best to have an emergency account. They say that it is best to have an account where you have at least six months saved to pay for all your bills just in case something happens. Take even a couple of dollars out of your paycheck, cut back on anything you need to, but it is important to do this. I had a lease on my cell phone; I finally paid that. It will save me a little bit. I set a payment on auto pay—again, more savings. It takes discipline, but I refuse to live paycheck-to-paycheck for the rest of my life. I don't have the latest phone or latest styles, but I am grateful for what I do have. If you need help, just reach out to your local banker and have them help you rebuild your credit or at least guide you. Some of you are doing business on your own and not getting credited for it. Seek advice from your accountant to see whether starting a business will help you when doing your taxes. You might be surprised.

To start a business, you need to get an EIN (employer identification number, also known as a Federal Tax Identification Number) on IRS.gov and set up for business in your state. It can be a sole proprietor, LLC, or corporation. Start keeping track of your expenses and your profits. I share this knowledge with you to hopefully help you, and then you can share the information with someone else.

Me losing my high credit made me very humble because I always prided myself on my good credit. When I say I lost it all, I mean I lost it all—not only my good credit, but also any financial comfort I had.

God heard my voice and still does. He hears my cry, and He answers me. He gave me a miracle two times that night. If He did it for me, He can do it for you. You just have to trust Him and give it to Him. He is our provider. I say this with tears in my eyes.

Since this happened, I have been able to refinance my home at a low rate, and now my home shows up on my credit report; I just have to work on the payments because my payment went up more than anticipated after my repairs and remodeling. I will share pictures of my home now and a picture of where I lived when I was young. To God be all the glory.

Chapter 15
MY MIRACLES

L et me share some of the miracles God has worked in my life so they may encourage you to believe in His promises and goodness.

1. When I was a child, during one of our trips back to Texas, we stopped at a rest area to sleep. We had a station wagon, and it was custom for several Mexican families to travel in caravans. It was dark, and the kids and I were outside playing touch. Your name would be called out, and you had to tag the other kids. If you touched the person, then they would be out. They were all calling out my name, "Sandra, here I am. Sandra, here." I heard my name all over the dark rest area. Meanwhile, the parents were in the vehicles trying to sleep because we had two more days of driving ahead.

   I heard my name being called repeatedly behind a wall of weeds. I asked who it was, and a man's voice said, "Come, Sandra." I walked closer to the voice, and then, all of a sudden, fear overtook my mind and body. Something told me to stop, and I ran toward my parents' vehicle, crying. They started counting heads, and all of the children were with us; none of them were behind that dark wall. What if I had not listened to that little voice I heard? I would have been abducted. Would I be alive today?

2. I have great respect for medical professionals, but based on my own experiences, I am here to tell you that you need to trust God first. I believe in miracles and the power of healing prayer. Surrender it to God if you are in a situation that you cannot control.

   When I was pregnant with my first baby, I was told by the doctor that I had to abort or I could die. I did not listen to him, and I said instead, "God, I am going to trust You now. Take me but not my baby." I delivered a healthy baby girl five weeks early. Here is a picture of my baby girl, Yvette, and another of us.

3. One Thanksgiving Day, my husband and I were in Florida at our home. That year was 2004, when three hurricanes hit Central Florida back to back to back: Hurricane Charlie, Hurricane Frances, and Hurricane Ivan. Every time there was a hurricane, we lost all of our food because we had no power for one week. We had not applied for any assistance, so we had no turkey dinner and no money. Yes, we both had jobs, but because we were middle class, we did not qualify for any assistance. We always blessed others over ourselves, so we had no money until the next paycheck.

   I could not help but to feel sad. It was a chilly morning that day. When I opened the door, I saw a paper bag full with a frozen turkey, mashed potatoes, and other items. I cried and later found out that a church had blessed us with this much-needed meal.

Yvette and I

4. God covered me again when the doctors told me my son was showing signs of having Down syndrome and they wanted me to abort him. Sounds familiar, right? I cried and worried if I was making the right decision, but I told God that I was going to trust Him. He brought me out of my past, and I was ready to continue my journey with Him. I proceeded with my pregnancy, and my son, Joshua, was born. Here is my boy, Joshua Emmanuel, with his sister. Yes, he was born healthy.

5. God saved my home. Some may not think this is a miracle, but I do because I do not take anything for granted. When I divorced, I walked away with nothing except debt and my home, which was drastically upside down with negative equity. By the grace of God, I have been able to make the many needed repairs. There is so much love in my home now because there is peace. After the living room was remodeled, my kids and I gravitated more to it. It just feels comfortable when before it did not. I always have a project going on, and my kitchen will be next. I am slowly replacing the floors, windows, and paint, and it feels great. In the process of my remodeling, I was able to bless so many people with furniture, tools, housewares, televisions, clothes, paintings, shoes, and so many other things. I have not finished with my remodeling, and I know it takes time; I am just grateful for what I have been able to do so far.

6. After having a minivan, in 2013, God blessed me with a 2007 Lexus that only had 14,000 miles on it. I drove around in my Lexus after my divorce, which

Yvette and Josh

My current four bedroom home

gave me peace of mind because I then felt safe to travel with my kids. The minivan I had previously had transmission problems, so I limited my traveling for safety reasons. I have put more than 100,000 miles on the Lexus and am grateful because this car has kept up with my traveling needs. It is now January 2020, and my car is 13 years old. I am just humbled and grateful that God provided a reliable car for me when I needed it most.

7. There is also the miracle of my dad coming back into my life. Here is a picture of my dad and me, and the next picture is of him, me, and his wife, America. The healing part is my miracle.

8. When I had my surgery in October 2018, I had little money because I had to pay for some medical expenses upfront. I had very little money and little food, and I did not know how I was going to make ends meet. My best friend came knocking on my door with bags of groceries, laundry soap, and juices. God is so good because He used my friend to bless me with what I needed to survive.

9. In December 2018, I was at Dr. Cindy Trimm's end-of-year gathering when I got a call from my kids that they had just been in a hit-and-run in their father's car on the main highway outside of Orlando. That Friday, I had left for Atlanta, and it just so happened that I was worshiping God all throughout the day, telling God that my answer to Him was YES.

    This is what my ex's car looked like after the accident. Joshua was in the backseat and Yvette in the front passenger seat. They walked out alive. I thank you, God.

Dad and I

My ex's car after the accident

10. One day, I will meet an amazing man who will be connected with me on every level. I thank God in advance for the humble, loving husband who is coming my way.

If I think back, many times I have been blessed. I am so grateful to all my friends and even to those who purposefully hurt me. All those experiences have molded me into being the woman that I am now. Women, hear me roar. I am confident, fearless, and I love life.

Chapter 16

SOWING SEED

I know everywhere we go we hear about sowing and tithing. What is said about sowing seed in the Bible?

The King James Version says, "But this I say, He which soweth sparingly shall also reap sparingly and he which soweth bountifully shall reap also bountifully" (2 Corinthians 9:6).

At first, I did not understand this, but I am here to share with you what I learned about sowing seeds. I am blessed because I sow. I may not have very much at times, but I make it a point to bless others. There are many stories I can share with you in which I obeyed the Holy Spirit and was blessed in return. Just recently, I heard the Holy Spirit tell me to give $100 to the cleaning lady. You know me—I am a single mom on a budget. I questioned, "Is this me hearing things, or is this really You, God?" I heard the instruction again, and I did not question it. I blessed the lady. The next day, I was blessed with three times the amount.

A while back, there was this lady from church who asked me if I had a dining table I could give her. I knew I was eventually going to get another one, but I was holding on to my current table until that day. I remember the day she asked; the Holy Spirit told me to give her the dinette set. I responded, "Lord, what am I going to use in the meantime? I don't have money to buy a new one."

I should have just obeyed, but nope. I am just being real before you think wrong of me. The next day, I heard the same thing: "Give her the set." I called the lady and told her to come pick it up as soon as she could. My kids and I ate on a fold-out table for about a month until the day came when I checked the mail and I got a large check. I cried and thanked God. It happened because I was finally obedient. I was able to buy a table and a sofa with that money.

I just want to encourage you to try and listen to the Holy Spirit. If you are being told to release something, then do it. God is faithful, and He loves us. He wants to bless us.

On May 5, 2018, I went to a conference in Fort Lauderdale, Florida. I met a woman there who has forever changed my life. She is prophetess Nicole. After the event, I came down from my room, and I approached her, introducing myself. She asked me to sit next to her, and she began to prophesy to me. She mentioned my book, and she told me to get myself checked out at the doctors. The ovarian cyst was diagnosed shortly after that encounter.

She said she saw a music symbol next to me, and she asked me if I gambled or went to casinos. I thought about it, and I said, "Well, I have been on one cruise ship, and I did play with the machines, but that was years ago." She asked if there was anything else. I said no, and then it hit me—I play the lottery, buying lotto quick picks all the time. I liked playing and did not know it was that serious until she said this. She said God had been delaying my blessing because if I won the lottery, He would not get the glory. There I was hoping to win some money, and I was stopping my blessings. I told her there was no need to worry, that effective immediately I would stop playing the lottery and gambling. I don't know about you, but I want what God has for me.

I want to live right and be blessed. What I want to do is to inspire you and give you hope. If God could do all this for me, He can do it for you. All you have to do is believe.

Chapter 17
NOTE TO MY FUTURE HUSBAND

Babe, I need you more than I care to admit it. I know you have not met me, yet I pray for you often. I ask God to give you patience and not give up on me, I am coming. I am sorry it has taken longer than I expected to find you. I was not ready, and God has been molding me into the woman I needed to be for you and for Him. I was a mess before, but now I am beautiful inside and out.

I hope you can laugh at my silly jokes since no one else does. I hope we can be best friends and be able to talk about everything. I will tell you in advance that I will need your help in the gym. I need a gym partner. So lift, babe, lift. I want to drop the weight so I can be healthy. As you probably read, I have two kids. We are a package deal. They are good kids. Do you have kids? Will we be a blended family? What are your favorite hobbies? I hope we can travel together, but most importantly, pray together.

Babe, just wait for me. I am coming. I promise to not disappoint you. We have a world to discover together. I look forward to meeting you and your family. Do you think your family will like me? I am nerdy but fun. I will continue to pray for you. Don't give up on me. I am coming, and we are going to lead many souls to Christ, so get ready.

Truly Yours,
Sandra Boyd

Chapter 18
MY JOURNAL

I am starting a short journal so that I cannot lose my focus because I am trying to change my trajectory. Join me in this journey because I believe in positive change.

Day 1

> *And be not conformed to this world: but be ye transformed*
> *by the renewing of your mind, that ye may prove what*
> *is that good, and acceptable, and perfect, will of God.*
> (Romans 12:2 KJV).

In order for me to be able to reinvent and renew myself, I need to change some behaviors. I have started deleting phone numbers and pictures. Yes, I said it—delete, delete, delete. Let's be real. Sometimes, we hang tight to things and people who do not deserve to be in our lives or whom God has warned us about. I am taking a breath, closing my eyes, and just giving it to God.

Question 1

What behavior or action will I do differently hoping for a better result?

_____

_____

_____

_____

_____

_____

_____

_____

_____

_____

_____

_____

_____

_____

_____

Day 2

Time to declutter and get organized. I just walked into my closet with a large, black trash bag. That's it—time to organize my closet. I've moved from one room to another, so my clothes are a mess. If I have not worn an item in a while or it does not fit, it is going into the bag.

I am going to donate the clothes. That does make me feel better. Now, I can see my closet has much more free room. This makes me feel better too because I can walk into my closet and see all of the floor. I was a mess before. I have found out that when I am struggling emotionally, my room and home are a reflection of me.

Question 2

What are you going to do differently to make you feel better?

_____

_____

_____

_____

_____

_____

_____

_____

_____

_____

_____

_____

_____

_____

_____

Day 3

I invested in myself today. I went and bought makeup. Nothing big—just makeup and a makeup bag were enough to make me happy. My daughter helped me organize my bag, and it is awesome. I am on day three of doing my full face even though we are wearing our masks.

Who would have thought that by doing something so simple, it would cause me to feel more confident and sexy? I like it.

Question 3

If you could buy yourself something or make something that makes you happy, what would it be? I would like to know, so please do share this with me.

_____
_____
_____
_____
_____
_____
_____
_____
_____
_____
_____
_____
_____
_____
_____
_____
_____
_____

Day 4

If any man defile the temple of God, him shall God destroy; for the temple of God is holy, which temple ye are. (1 Corinthians 3:17)

Here is what I understood of this: my body is the temple of God. So, my body is holy. Have I really treated my body as holy? No, I have not. Now that I am trying to align myself with my destiny, I need to do a better job with my body.

I have started this week by limiting my eating out. I pass by the fast food restaurants in the morning, and it is hard because I am hungry. I had the opportunity to cook at home, and I did. I have started making frozen smoothies. I will let you know how that turns out.

I want to transform my body, and I understand it takes time, so I will keep you posted.

Question 4

How are you defiling your body? What can you do differently?

_____
_____
_____
_____
_____
_____
_____
_____
_____
_____

Day 5

Time to hit the gym. I will start by walking for thirty minutes a day and by doing weights. Tomorrow will be my leg day.

I should see some progress in my body once this becomes part of my weekly habits. I am committing to start by going to the gym three days a week. My kids are pushing me to go so let's do this.

Question 5

Are you able to go to a gym or work out at home? Do you have a friend that can be your accountability partner?

_____

_____

_____

_____

_____

_____

_____

_____

_____

_____

_____

_____

_____

_____

_____

_____

_____

_____

_____

Day 6

I need to have a prayer space in my home. This will allow me to limit the distractions and just focus and have my quiet time with God.

I remember I used to get on my knees and pray more often, so I am going back to this. Let's plan for it.

Question 6

Do you plan to pray or do it out of the blue? I am asking you to be intentional with me. Let's plan that for the next ten days we set time aside to pray. So below write down how you will make it happen. If you want to Zoom or Facetime for prayer, I am game. Let's do it. Find me on social media.

_____

_____

_____

_____

_____

_____

_____

_____

_____

_____

_____

_____

_____

_____

_____

_____

Day 7

Choose your friends wisely. This is day seven of the first week of reinventing myself. I have deleted some numbers off my cell phone of people who were negative or whom I was tempted by.

The new eating habits I have started are starting to pay off. I am beginning to feel a difference in how my tops fit. I am starting to walk sexier. I also started drinking a cup of warm water with lemon juice to help me in my weight loss. According to Edison Institute of Nutrition, drinking lemon with water on an empty stomach has weight loss benefits and other numerous benefits.

One thing to keep in mind is that we all have people in our past who, the minute you start doing well, are going to come back into your life. Maybe their purpose is to derail you, but—guess what—we are sharp and wise. Pray about your friendships.

Remember to see the clues and discern that. It is okay to distance myself if it means self-preservation, but I am not better than anyone. I am a sinner, and my goal is to be a better person that does not judge others.

Question 7

Do you know who your friends are? Pray for discernment in that area.

_____

_____

_____

_____

_____

_____

_____

_____

Day 8

Now that I have decided who is in my inner circle, I am asking myself if friends motivate me. Do they push me to be a better person, or do they just agree with everything I say just to avoid confrontation?

I do not need a "yes person"; I need a friend. I can't count the times I was not living right and my friends checked me on it. Honesty is the best, even if it hurts.

Sometimes, we trust the wrong people. Going forward, I will not share all of my intimate feelings with people who may take advantage of it.

Question 8

Do you have any friends that hurt you because they know so much about you? If you do, forgive them and learn that this is a new day. What will you do differently here?

_____

_____

_____

_____

_____

_____

_____

_____

_____

_____

_____

_____

_____

_____

_____

_____

Day 9

I set this day to book appointments for my wellness. In the past, I put myself last, and I did not take care of myself.

I have to change this about myself. I need to focus on myself. I am worthy, and people depend on me. My kids need their mother to be around for many years. I want to be around for many years to come, so I am setting up my appointments and not making any excuses.

Question 9

Are you up to date with all your checkups and appointments? Physical, vision, dental. Annual mammograms, colon tests, therapist, massage, you name it. If not, use the space below to start writing down what you need to get done.

_____

_____

_____

_____

_____

_____

_____

_____

_____

_____

_____

_____

_____

_____

_____

_____

_____

Day 10

Remember the part about me deleting old phone numbers and pictures? Well, part of that is so my mindset will change. No more meaningless dating and sex. Yes, I said it. I am not pretending to be innocent. I get it, trust me. I have asked God for companionship for years now, and I do not have that, so what happened? I was caught up in the lust of the flesh when what I desired was companionship.

No more. I am worthy of waiting for the right person. I am worthy of a man who will love me for me without asking me to hook up on the first night or second or third, etc.

Repeat out loud, "Lord, I know You know my weaknesses. Help me be strong so I can wait on who You have for me. This time, it will not be me who decides who I am with. Send him to me, Lord; I trust You. Send me the man who will love me regardless of my past. In Jesus's name, I pray, Amen."

Do not defile your body.

If any man defile the temple of God, him shall God destroy: for the temple of God is holy, which temple ye are. Let no man deceive himself. If any man among you seemth to be wise in this world, let him become a fool, that he may be wise. (1 Corinthians 3:17-19 KJV)

Question 10

How will you change your mindset?

_____

_____

_____

_____

_____

_____

_____

Day 11

Start a purpose board. I started mine, and I only have a few things on it now, but I am adding more. I have also placed it on my desk so that I see it every day. It will be my constant reminder of what I want to accomplish. In my case, finishing this book and spreading the gospel are key to me. I also started studying to get my investment licenses. One day in the future, I want to work on getting a doctorate in divinity. All of this will be on my purpose board.

Question 11

What will you put on your purpose board? Write down some words or ideas that are important to you so that these can be put on your purpose board.

_____

_____

_____

_____

_____

_____

_____

_____

_____

_____

_____

_____

_____

_____

_____

_____

Chapter 19
MY FIRST PODCAST

Finally, my book was printed and I was so excited that I put a picture of it up on a social media platform. I was contacted by an international best-selling author and podcaster. You can imagine my excitement. I was surprised and elated when I got his email. I went to work and told all my coworkers about it. They were so happy for me, and I kept saying, "God, use me for your glory". From his email and website, I got the impression that the podcaster was a busy man and in high demand. The time came, and he contacted me via audio. He explained to me what was going to happen. Prior to doing our podcast, he asked me what the book was about. I told him that it was about how God saved me and that it was about my testimony.

He told that if I wanted to make it big and be able to make money off of my speaking engagements, then I was to not mention Jesus or speak of religion. He said that some people do not like to hear of Jesus Christ or of religion. I listened to him in utter disbelief of what I had just heard.

He continued to share his experience of how he had made less than $100 during his first speaking engagement and that now his fee was above $20,000 for his appearance and speeches. He said he never mentions religion or God even though he grew up believing.

Let me be very direct so that you know where I stand in this matter. When the podcaster started recording, he asked me, "Sandra, what is your book about?"

I replied, "It is about how God saved my life. It is about my testimony with Jesus Christ." He paused and changed the questions to be more about my banking career. The bottom line is he was asking me to deny God for money. Now, I know this may rub some people the wrong way; understand that I am just the messenger.

Matthew 10:33

But everyone who denies me here on earth, I will also deny before my Father in heaven. (Matthew 10:33)

Chapter 20

THE SEASON OF THE PRODIGAL SON

The season of the prodigal sons and daughters is here. A prodigal is a person who leaves home and behaves recklessly, but later makes a repentant return. My past is my past. I have moved forward with it and left the past behind. I have been washed new because Jesus died on the cross for my sins.

Stop beating yourself up; this is your time to move forward. I know you are destined for greatness. All those times you read posts of warriors, of "be the chosen," this is why the enemy attacked you hard: he saw your potential and your destiny. There are people that need to hear your story so that they too can be set free. Don't be selfish and keep your testimony to yourself.

How can you start the change?

- Step 1: Repent.
- Step 2: Ask God to come into your life.
- Step 3: Start forgiving those who hurt you and forgive yourself.
- Step 4: Don't look back.

ABOUT THE AUTHOR

Sandra Boyd has dedicated her life to helping others and empowering them financially. She has earned a reputation among her peers as a catalyst for change and a positive thinker. Sandra endured many painful situations and gives others hope so they too can press forward. Her mantra is "If God did it for me, He can do it for you."